GYPS

By the same author in Piccolo

TALES FROM THE GALAXIES
(with Michael Pearson)

CONDITIONS OF SALE

This book shall not, by way of trade or otherwise, be lent, re-sold, hired out or otherwise circulated without the publisher's prior consent in any form of binding or cover other than that in which it is published and without a similar condition including this condition being imposed on the subsequent purchaser. The book is published at a net price and is supplied subject to the Publishers Association Standard Conditions of Sale registered under the Restrictive Trade Practices Act, 1956.

GYPSY FOLK TALES

AMABEL WILLIAMS-ELLIS

A Piccolo Original

PAN BOOKS LTD : LONDON

First published 1973 by Pan Books Ltd,
33 Tothill Street, London SW1

ISBN 0 330 23741 1

This collection © Amabel Williams-Ellis 1973

Printed in Great Britain by
Richard Clay (The Chaucer Press), Ltd, Bungay, Suffolk

Contents

1	The Leaves that Hung but Never Grew	7
2	The Three Sisters	15
3	The Boy and his Club	22
4	The Basket-maker's Donkey	29
5	The Squirrel and the Fox	32
6	The Little Crop-tailed Hen	44
7	Twopence Halfpenny	55
8	Appy Boswell's Monkey	64
9	The Maid of the Mill	66
10	Goggle-eyes	79
11	The Green Man of No Man's Land	89
12	Down Underground	102
13	The King of the Herrings	105
14	The Red King and the Witch	114
	Afterword	124
	Notes	127

Acknowledgements

'The Leaves that Hung but Never Grew', 'The Three Sisters', 'The Boy and his Club', 'The Squirrel and the Fox', 'Twopence Halfpenny', 'The Maid of the Mill', 'Goggle-eyes', 'The Green Man of No Man's Land' and 'The King of the Herrings' first appeared in *Welsh Gypsy Folk Tales*, collected by John Sampson (The Gregynog Press, 1933); 'The Basket-maker's Donkey', 'The Little Crop-tailed Hen', 'Appy Boswell's Monkey' and 'Down Underground' first appeared in *Gypsy Folk Tales* by Dora Yates (Phoenix House, 1948); and 'The Red King and the Witch' first appeared in *Rumanian Gypsy Stories* by Francis Hindes-Groome (Hurst & Blackett, 1899).

1

The Leaves that Hung but Never Grew

A little lonely house, and a mother and her daughter living there. They were as poor as poor could be, and the girl went to look for work.

Away she went, and she came to a lordly mansion. The nobleman asked her what she wanted. He called her in.

'I am looking for work.'

'I will give you work.'

The task he gave her was to find 'the leaves that hung but never grew'.

Off she went to seek she didn't know what. Those who saw her saw a lovely young woman on the road, looking troubled about something.

She journeyed on until she found a little cottage. She knocked at the door and out came an old witch. The young girl asked for work and the old witch bade her come into the parlour. She saw a great black boar chained in one corner.

The old witch made some good tea for her, and

gave her plenty to eat. She ate her fill, and made an end of her meal.

The only work which the old witch gave her was to look after this black boar. The girl tended the boar for weeks. She knew not how to set about asking the old witch concerning the leaves. There was a witch-daughter in the place too, but she didn't know how to ask her either.

She grew weary and discontented. One day she said to the black boar:

'Oh boar, boar! See my hands now! They were white and delicate when I came here; but look how rough and dirty are they now and all through looking after you!'

'Wait a while,' said he, 'I warrant you, you'll soon find yourself turned into a black sow in the other corner.'

She said nothing in reply.

'Why have you come here?' the boar asked her one day.

'I came to seek "*the leaves that hung but never grew*".'

No sooner was the word spoken about the leaves than the boar was changed into a young gentleman.

'Go upstairs into the witch's bedchamber,' says he, 'and put your hand under her pillow. You will find a little wallet there. When your

There was an old witch there, and a great black boar

hand touches the leaves that are in it, wish that the witch may stay asleep and not waken.'

She went upstairs, she laid her hand upon the wallet, and she willed the witch to stay asleep and not waken. She took the wallet and came downstairs. She gave half the leaves to the young gentleman.

'Now,' said he, 'let us get ready the three enchantments for the witch when she wakes and asks whether you are coming to bed.

'First, you must wish that the poker shall say, "I am raking out the fire." Then that the broom shall say, "I am sweeping the room." Lastly, that the chair shall say: "I am coming up now."'

The girl wished these three things and after that the two fled away together.

Lo, the witch wakes up. She calls the girl to come to bed. The poker answers, 'I am raking out the fire.'

After a while she calls the girl again, but the broom answers, 'I am sweeping the room.'

She calls her once more; the chair answers, 'I am coming now.'

The girl didn't come, so the witch called again. There was no answer.

The witch was furious. She guessed that the girl and the young gentleman had escaped. She called the witch, her daughter, and told her to follow them and whatsoever she saw on the way, to bring it home with her.

Lo, the two are speeding on their way. After a while they see the witch's daughter coming after them like the wind. She had almost overtaken them . . .

Said the gentleman to the maiden: 'Wish yourself a duck, and me a running stream; when she tries to catch you, dive under the water.' So the youth was transformed into a running stream, and the girl turned herself into a duck.

And now the witch's daughter overtakes them. She approaches the duck; she tries to catch her. 'Duck, duck, pretty little duck,' calls the witch's daughter, 'have you seen anyone pass by this way?' No answer, and every time she came close, the little duck dived under the water.

The witch's daughter went home and told her mother that she had seen a little duck swimming on the water, and nought else.

'Those were they!' cried the old witch. 'Go back, and fetch me just one feather from the duck, and I will very soon have them back again.'

The witch's daughter set off again to get the feather. This time she saw neither duck nor stream. Both had vanished. She was heartbroken. She went home and told the old witch that she could find nothing.

The two had hurried away until they reached a fork of the road. Here they must part from one another. They agreed that he should go to his home and return again to her. Said the girl to the youth: 'When you get home, don't let your kindred kiss you, or you will forget me.'

The young man went home. His family had not seen him for years, not for all the time he had been a black boar in the witch's house. His brothers and sisters caressed him and kissed him, and so it was that he forgot all about the young maiden.

The girl waited long at the fork of the road. At last she felt sure that his kindred had kissed him, and that she was forgotten. She went home to her mother, to the poor little cottage where she had always lived. Two days passed.

The nobleman from the lordly mansion came to find out whether she had found the leaves.

'You have come home, young woman,' says he.

'Yes,' says she, and she put her hand in a casket and pulled out the leaves. The lord knew them as soon as he saw them.

Now someone had offered a great reward to whoever should find these leaves; but this poor girl knew nothing about it. The lord wanted the money for his own daughter.

Now he had the leaves, he thought how to get rid of this poor girl. He invited her to the mansion to take tea, and her mother expected her to return home with much money, but the nobleman had planned to take her life. When they had all had tea he lodged her in a fine room with a bed to herself. Above her head was a sort of canopy set with iron spikes, and this was to fall on her and kill her while she slept. It was to make a great noise when it fell, so that the nobleman might know that she was killed.

Lo – midnight now. The clock struck the hour. The girl awoke. She saw this canopy gradually coming down on her. She thought of the leaves. When she thought of the leaves, she thought of the young man. She drew from her pocket one leaf that she had kept back, and immediately he stood before her.

She sprang up and gave him her hand – not a word spoken.

He told her softly to will them all to sleep. She willed them to sleep.

'Now then,' says he, 'let us begone.' He went to the door and opened it. The two stole away and no one saw or heard them go. All was still.

'I am afraid to live with my mother,' said she to him, 'I must go further away, where the nobleman cannot find me.'

'So be it! I will go with you, go where you will,' said the young gentleman.

He took her to his own home.

'Now at last,' said the young man, 'we have a place where we can talk undisturbed. Shall we two wed?'

'That is the very thing I myself desire,' said the young woman, and again she gave him her hand.

The youth told the coachman to harness the horses to the carriage. They drove away to London. And in London they were married. Then they came back again to Wales. They kept a mill beside the sea and lived there happily from that day to this.

A big pudding for me for telling you this lie!

2

The Three Sisters

There was a cottage and there lived in this cottage an old man and his wife. They had three children, and these three children were three little sisters. And they lived there summer after summer until their father and mother died.

And two summers after that there came to the cottage a little old woman who wore a red cloak. And she went to the door and begged for a cup of tea.

'No,' said the eldest sister, 'we haven't enough for ourselves.'

'I will bind your head and your eyes, if I don't bind your whole body,' said the crone to her. With that she went away.

And now these three sisters grew poor. And one day the eldest sister said to the other two: 'I am going to look for work. You two stay here to look after the house. But if you see the spring dried up and blood in the handle of the dipper that we use to ladle out the water, it will mean that evil has befallen me. Then, one of you, come to search for me.'

And so each day, in the morning, when they got up, the two sisters who stayed at home used to look for these tokens.

The eldest sister journeyed far, and further yet, to where the devil never wound his horn and the cock never crew. Night fell. Presently she saw a little man in a red jerkin. She didn't know it, but this little red-jerkin'd fellow was brother to the old woman of the red cloak. And before the girl had asked him anything, he put a question to her.

'Are you looking for work?'

'Yes,' said the girl.

Little Red Jerkin gave her no hint of the trials that lay before her. He opened a gate: 'Go up there, and you'll get work!'

Up she climbed. There were little white stones along by the path all the way up the hill. 'Stop and look!' cried one white stone.

The girl stopped and looked at the stone. She was bewitched into a trance and changed into a white stone.

That, you see, was how old Red Cloak did as she'd said. She has bound the girl's head and eyes with a spell; she has bound her whole body.

The next morning, at home at the cottage, the

second sister got up and went to the door. She opened the door and there was the spring dried up and blood in the handle of the dipper that they used to ladle out the water. Horror came over her when she saw these things.

'Some evil has befallen our sister,' she called out to the youngest girl. Then the spring flowed and the dipper was bright again.

Now she, in her turn, said to her younger sister: 'If you see the spring dried up and blood on the dipper, some misfortune has overtaken me. Come then, and look for me.'

So now the second sister journeyed to where the devil never wound his horn and the cock never crew, until she too met this man in the red jerkin. And before she could utter a word to him, Red Jerkin spoke to her:

'Are you looking for work?' asked he.

'No,' answered the girl, 'I am looking for my sister.'

'Your sister is up there; she has found work, and is doing well.'

The gate was opened and the girl climbed up the hill.

'Stop!' cried one white stone. The girl did not pause, but went straight on.

'Look!' called another pebble to her. But the girl went on.

'Look! Here is your sister!' cried a third stone.

She stood still and looked round when she heard this about her sister. And then she too was bewitched into a magic trance, and turned into a white stone.

The youngest sister was alone at home now. She got up one morning and went to the door and opened it. There was no water in the spring; it was dried up. There was blood in the dipper! Then the youngest sister burst into tears. But she had more spirit than the other two. She knew not where they had gone: she knew not where to look for them. But, after fastening the door, she took the road on which she had seen her two sisters set out.

So she too journeyed far and further yet, to where the devil never wound his horn and the cock never crew, until she too met the little fellow in the red jerkin. Before he could open his mouth, the youngest sister spoke to him. This time it was the girl that got in first. She asked him about work.

'Yes, there is work for you.' But this time Red Jerkin's heart was well-nigh broken, because the maiden had got in the first word. He opened the gate and the girl climbed up the hill. As she climbed, one white stone cried out to her, 'Stop!'

The girl went on.

This time it was the youngest sister that spoke first

'Look!' cried a second stone.

'This is the place!' cried a third stone.

The maiden was quite fearless. She paid no heed to them.

'Look, here are your two sisters!' cried yet another stone.

'Kiss them then,' said she, and on she went, never stopping until there were no more stones or pebbles and she reached the little old woman in the red cloak.

When Red-Cloak saw the girl she fell on her knees before her.

'Have you found me then, little lady?'

'I have,' said the girl – the little lady.

And now, lo and behold! All that sleepy and slumbrous spell was broken. And all these white stones and pebbles got back their former shapes. It was this maiden who had broken the whole enchantment. The girl – the little lady – wasn't afraid, and she went to her two sisters and led them up to the old woman in the red cloak.

'Here are my two sisters,' said she.

'I know them,' answered Red-Cloak. 'But it is you, my little lady, who are mistress here now. All is left in your hands. Do as you will.'

'I thank you, good aunt,' she answered.

Red-Cloak showed the youngest sister where a great hoard of treasure was hidden. Then the girl gave her two sisters each a bagful of gold, and told them to send her word if any danger should ever again befall them. And they both fell on their knees before their youngest sister. They were escorted home. And she became the greatest lady in all that land, far and wide, and she married Red Jerkin, who had become a tall, handsome young fellow. And they live there happily to this day.

3

The Boy and his Club

There was a cottage and an old woman and her son. They were so miserably poor that the landlord had to come for the rent time after time.

The old woman had three cows and nothing else besides. She said to her son:

'Let us sell the three cows at the fair tomorrow, so that I may pay the rent.'

The boy set off with the cows. He met a man on the road.

'Where are you going with those cows?' the man asked.

'To the fair to sell them.'

'Sell them to me,' says the man.

'What will you give me for them?'

'A club, a musical box and this little bee.'

The boy took them and went back home.

'What did you get for the cows?' asked his old mother.

'These three things,' said her son and showed them to the old woman.

The club, the musical box and the little bee

'How foolishly you've behaved!' said she, and she scolded him soundly. He pulled out the musical box and made it play, which made the old woman dance until she was too tired to stand.

'Do but stop playing, my boy, and I will never scold you again.'

The following day the landlord came for his rent.

'I know what to do,' said the boy. He called to the club. 'Lay on, club, lay on!' said he. The club drubbed the man out of the house.

Said the son to his mother, 'I am going to seek my fortune.' Lo! He sets out with the club and the bee, but he left the musical box with his mother.

He walked for a long, long way. He saw a great castle, but it was only half-built. Every day the workmen built it up, and every night it was pulled down. The lord of it had proclaimed that he would give his daughter to the man who should find out who pulled the castle down.

The boy gathered together a heap of stones by the wayside, and lay down behind this wall to watch the castle. He watched for a long time. Midnight came: it struck twelve. He saw two giants go up to the castle to pull it down, one on this side and one on the other. The boy took a stone in his hand, and hurled it at one of the giants.

'What art thou doing?' said this giant to the other.

'I am doing naught!'

The boy hurled yet another stone, and hit one giant on the back.

'Don't bump against me,' said this giant to the other.

'I did naught; why dost talk like that?'

So a great quarrel broke out between the two giants. They fell a-fighting until they killed each other. The boy cut off the heads of the two giants, and carried one away with him to show to the lord. He hurried off to the grand mansion in which the lord lived to tell the lord that he had found out who had been pulling down the castle. He showed the giant's head and asked the lord for his daughter.

The lord did not like to give his daughter to such a poor man.

'There are three more things that must be done before I give her to you. Tomorrow you must catch the old witch who lives in the forest.' He gave the boy plenty to eat and drink, and a good bed to sleep in.

He slept all night. He got up early in the morning and took a two-handed auger with him into the forest. He bored a big hole in a tree with the auger, and waited close by until the witch should come. Soon he saw her – a small hideous old witch with long, long hair. She looked at the hole. She was surprised.

'Who made this hole?' muttered she to herself.

The boy came up. He bade the witch good day.

'What is that door in the tree?' she asked.

'It leads into a pretty little house that I have made for you. You will be snug in that little house; neither frost nor snow will find you there.'

The old witch came right up to the tree. The boy seized her hair in his hand, pulled it through the hole, and tied it round the tree. Then he bound her arms and carried her off, tree and all. He delivered her to the lord, and they put her in a cage outside the mansion. And there she stayed for years, spitting upon all the servant girls who passed.

'Now then, my boy, I want you to catch the wild boar and bring him to me.'

'That's nothing,' said the boy. 'I will do that tomorrow.' He went to bed and slept well. In the morning he got up and took with him a rope and some victuals which gave off a savoury smell. He laid the victuals under a tree and climbed the tree to hide himself. The boar soon scented the savoury smell: presently the boy heard him galloping through the forest. The boar came right up to the tree. Lo! He is eating now. The boy threw the rope round his snout, and pulled it tight.

'Well, there he is,' said the boy. 'I have got him now.' And he brought him home to the lord of the castle.

'I have still one more thing for you to do,' said the lord. 'You must go down into the lions' den: if the lions don't eat you, you shall have my daughter.' They flung the boy into the den, and he pulled out his club.

'Lay on, club, lay on!' he cried. And the club beat the lions to smithereens. All the people were dumbfounded: and the boy told them to lower a ladder for him. They were terrified of the club, so they lowered the ladder. He climbed up and let loose his bee. It stung the lord and all his fine friends who were there, until they were glad to beg for mercy. The lord saw that his daughter was now bound to belong to the boy, so he gave her to him.

The two were married and set off to visit his old mother. They came to the little cottage where the old woman lived. They knocked at the door. No one heard them. The boy burst it open and went in. There he saw his old mother lying on the flagstones. She was nearly dying of hunger. They called the doctor; the doctor gave her a little brandy, and she soon came to herself. The son took the old mother and his bride to the castle that had been half pulled down. And the lord gave it to them for their very own. And as far as I know, they are living there still.

Ask me no more to tell you any lies!

4

The Basket-maker's Donkey

Once upon a time, when the most part of gypsies used to travel with pack-donkeys, there was an old man that had had the same donkey for years and years, and as he'd had it for so long it was a great pet of his.

Well, one day this man was at home, making a basket or two for his wife to take round with her when she went calling. This was mostly what his occupation was – basket-making; though sometimes he'd cut a few pegs or a gross or two o' skewers. You know the sort of man; not one of our class of people, but he could talk a bit of Romany, and in a way of speaking you might call him a gypsy.

Well, as I was saying, this old man was at home one day, busying himself weaving a basket. And the donkey was with him just as it often was, only instead of just keeping him company as it used to do, it was bothering him all the while – first one way, then another; making itself a regular nuisance, it was! He drove it away three or four times, aye, more than that, but no sooner had he settled down to his basket making than it was back again. So at last he gets right angry with it, and picks up a long switch that's lying handy. He chases it with this, and as soon as he gets up with it he lets fly for all he's worth. It was a tidy big welt he caught it, I can tell you. He cut it clean in two from head to tail, and the two halves tumbled to the ground, the one this way, the other the opposite.

When the old man saw what he'd gone and done he was fair beside himself, him being so mortal fond of the donkey, and not having another to take his bits of things about.

'What can I do?' he says, 'what can I do?' An' the tears were rolling down his face.

'Oh, whatever can I do?' he says. Then he bethinks himself, all of a sudden like, of the willow withes he has for the basket making, and he runs and fetches an armful. And he stands the two halves of the donkey up, and he fits the one to the other, and binds the two halves together with the willow withes.

Then he goes and gets some clay, and he daubs it all along the joining; caulks the two halves together, he does! 'There now,' he says, 'I reckon I've made a good job of that.'

An' he had an' all, for the two halves of the donkey grew together again, an' he'd many a year's service out of it after that: in fact, it lasted him his life. What is more, the willow withes took root and grew as well. So, ever after, whenever he wanted to make a basket, he didn't have to go searching for withes; he always had a stock ready to hand!

5

The Squirrel and the Fox

There was a little village down in England, and two brothers living there. They were as poor as poor could be; they knew not what to do.

They went to look for work, but no work could they find. Said one to the other: 'There is a little old woman who lives down yonder in a small cave. Let us go there. The old woman will tell us whether there is good fortune before us.'

'Yes, let us go,' replied the other.

They came to the little dwelling, and halloo'd to the old woman. The old woman knew that they were coming and what they wanted. There was a great stone in front of the door. The old woman told them to drag away the stone. When they had dragged it away, she said: 'Carry me outside and set me on the stone, and I will tell you everything.'

The old woman had neither arms nor legs. She had been born so.

'Listen, both of you, to what I am going to tell you.'

Then said the armless one to Jack: 'Here is a little stone for thee.' (It was no bigger than an old-fashioned penny.) 'Keep this and do not take it out of the handkerchief until you come to three roads.'

The two brothers journeyed on. They reached these crossroads – three roads to choose. They halted and Jack pulled the little stone out of the handkerchief. He looked at it. One side of the stone was yellow as gold and the other side as black as coal.

'What are we to do with this stone?' he asked his brother.

No sooner was the word uttered than he heard something whisper in his ear: 'Toss it high in the air. If the stone falls at thy feet with the gold side uppermost, take the road on the right hand; and if it falls with the black side uppermost, take the road on the left hand.'

He tossed the stone high in the air, and it fell at his feet with the gold side uppermost. Jack said to his brother: 'You are to take the road to the left, and I will take the road to the right.'

Now the two sat down and had a talk together.

'I go where I go!' said Jack. 'Remember to come to where these three roads meet, in a year and a day; and if you get here before me, wait here for me: and if I arrive before you I will wait for you – if I'm alive.'

They set off.

It was a hot summer's day. Jack tramped mile after mile. He could see no house and night set in. He walked all night till morning.

Now he hears dogs barking: he stands still to listen. He goes on a little further. He sees a giant beside a tree and hears a young woman weeping. She was crying: 'Stop, Father! Leave me alone. Do not treat me thus!' She was the giant's daughter. The giant was about to put a rope around her neck; he meant to hang her. The giant wanted her to marry a certain man, but the young woman did not love him.

What did Jack do? He took the gold and black stone – the magic stone – and struck the giant on the head and killed him.

What did the young woman say to Jack?

'If you bury my father somewhere in a secret place where no one can find him, I will give you as much gold as you can carry away with you.'

'Good!' said Jack. 'I will lay him where none can find him.'

He was about to bury him when he found the little stone still stuck in the giant's head. He heard something whisper in his ear, 'Leave him where he is, and put the stone at his left foot, and he will never be seen again.'

Now they both go to the giant's house. The young woman opens a cupboard: in it were a great many bags of gold. She gives one of them to Jack, who puts it on his shoulder and goes away.

Lo! He travels over lofty mountains until he reaches the sea. He is weary and the bag that he carries is heavy. He sits down and sleeps for three or four hours.

He wakes and finds a man coming towards him with a great sack on his back. The man came up to him. He recognized him. He stared at him.

'Good heavens! You are my brother!'

'Yes, I am your brother, and I am weary.' He sat down and opened his great sack. It was a sack of food: 'I am hungry as well. I am going to eat!'

'And I am hungry too,' replied Jack.

'Why don't you eat then?' said the other.

'I have naught to eat.'

'What is in your sack?'

'Nothing but gold.'

'Then if you have gold, buy your food.'

'Gladly,' said Jack, 'give me my fill.'

'I will give you your fill if you give me a hatful of gold.' Jack opened the sack and filled his brother's hat with golden sovereigns. His brother gave him a little bread and meat.

The two travelled on together beside the seashore. They tramped for miles and miles. They met no one. They grew hungry again. They sat down, but Jack had to give his brother another hatful of coins before he would give him anything to eat.

And in this way they went on until they rested again. They had not much food left and now the brother would not give Jack anything to eat.

'You have got all my money,' said poor Jack, 'I have no more; and if you will not give me a morsel of food, I shall die of hunger.'

'No, I have told you, I shall give you nothing unless you pay for it.'

'I have nothing left to give you.'

'I will tell you what I will do with you,' said his brother. 'Give me the sight of one of your eyes and I will give you a little food.'

Jack gave it to him. Now he could only see out of one of his eyes. His brother gave him a little food. They finished their meal.

Another day passed. Jack was afraid to ask his brother to give him something to eat. He grew hungrier and hungrier. At last he asked his brother to give him a morsel of food.

'Not I,' said the brother, 'I haven't much left.

If you want any more give me the sight of your other eye.'

Jack gave it to his brother. His brother gave him a tiny morsel of food.

Poor Jack was blind now. The other brother had taken all the gold and now he went off leaving Jack alone.

Jack didn't know what to do. He crawled along on his hands and knees. He did not know whether it was day or whether it was night. He crept under a big tree. He did not care whether he lived or died.

'If I am to die I will die here.'

Presently he heard creatures in the tree above his head. And who were they? A Squirrel and a Fox, talking together. Jack found that he could understand their talk.

These two were in the habit of meeting here once a twelvemonth to tell each other the chief discoveries of the year. Jack listened.

Said the Fox to the Squirrel: 'There is a great city four miles on the other side of the mountain, and all the people there are dying of thirst. The water is dried up. And if they only knew it,' the Fox went on, 'if they were to dig a well near the town clock they would find enough water for three towns.'

'And have you heard, you old Goose-stealer,'

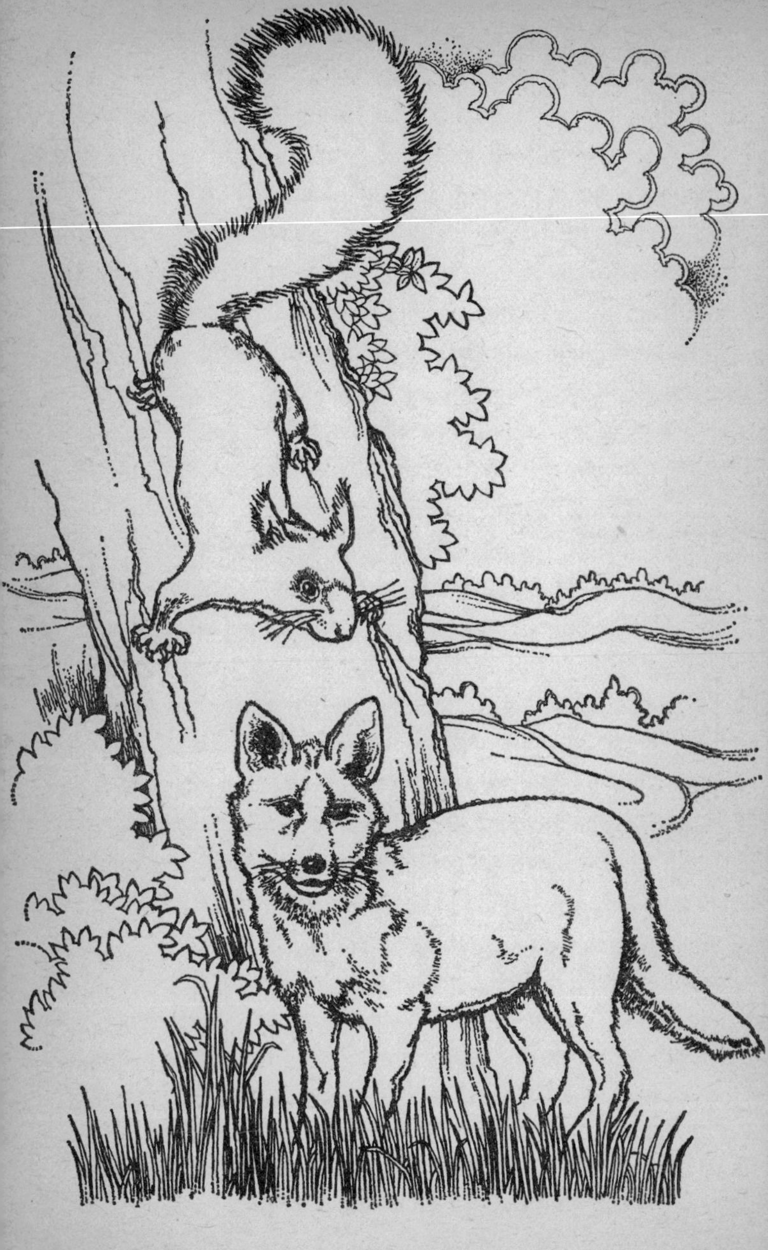

said the Squirrel, 'that the Lord Mayor of that place lost his sight last week?'

'Not I,' said the Fox, 'I have heard nothing of it. But do you see this leaf, White-tail?'

'Yes,' said the Squirrel.

'What fools the people of those parts are! If they were to rub the blind man's eyes with this kind of leaf, he would get back his sight.'

'Wait a moment, Sir Fox! I will tell you something.'

'Let me hear it,' said the Fox.

'In the same town there is a princess with two horns growing out of her forehead.'

'Well,' said the Fox, 'If they were to give her apples the horns would grow bigger, and if they were to give her oranges the horns would dwindle away. There's a reward offered by the Queen to whoever rids her of them.'

Of course Jack, this poor blind fellow beneath the tree, was listening to everything they said. Presently the Fox leapt down and the Squirrel scampered after him. Jack rose, took a few of the leaves and rubbed his eyes with them. As soon as he rubbed them, lo! he got his sight back. He was astounded.

'Well, I'll be off to the city now,' thinks Jack.

He crossed the mountain and came to the city. Somehow, he managed to dress himself up as a

There were a squirrel and a fox talking together

doctor, and went to the Hall where the blind Mayor lived. He knocked at the door and was invited inside by a manservant.

'I am a doctor come to restore the blind Lord Mayor's eyesight,' he said. He was taken upstairs. There was the Lord Mayor sitting in his easy-chair. Jack drew near to examine his eyes. He asked for what he needed; boiled the leaves he had brought and bottled them; dipped a feather in the bottle, and passed this feather twice across the Lord Mayor's eyes. The Lord Mayor regained his sight. He was so pleased that he didn't know how to reward the doctor enough. He gave Jack what he asked.

'Wait a moment,' said Jack, 'there is one thing I should like to do before I leave the Hall. I understand, my Lord Mayor, that the water in your town is dried up?'

'In truth, it is dried up.'

'Come with me and I will show you where there is plenty of water.' As soon as the Lord Mayor heard that, he ran up to Jack and clasped him to his breast.

'If you find water for us, I will give you three bags of gold pieces.' They went out and Jack led him up to the town clock.

'Do you see this spot? Bring your men here.'

'I will bring them at once.'

'Now then,' said Jack, 'dig down here.'

The men took off their coats – stripped down for the job. They dug down a little way. They found enough water for three towns. The Lord Mayor paid Jack, and Jack took the money.

'I'm doing so well in this town,' said he to himself, 'but I still have the King's daughter to deal with.'

Then he bought a basketful of apples and a basketful of oranges. He set them down close by the gate of the palace, and he waited there for three days.

On the third day the old King and Queen and their daughter came out in their chariot. The girl had two horns growing out of her head. The young lady cast her eye on the apples:

'Mother, look at those beautiful apples over there!'

'Would you like a few of them, daughter?'

'Yes,' said the young lady.

They bought some. The young lady ate a few that day. She got up the next morning and looked in her mirror. The horns had grown bigger. The King's daughter was horrified!

Jack disguised himself again as a doctor, and went to visit her a few days later.

'Welcome, Doctor; I am glad to see you,' said the princess. 'You see these horns on my forehead: do you know of anything that will make them smaller?'

'Yes,' said Jack. 'But you must give me money.'

'You shall have it,' said she.

Jack pulled an orange out of his pocket, cut a slice from it with his knife and went up to the princess.

'Open your mouth, young lady, put out your tongue.' He placed the slice on her tongue.

'Swallow that; I will return tomorrow morning.' The doctor took his leave.

Now it was morning again. The young lady got up and looked in her mirror. Both horns seemed smaller. The doctor paid her another visit. The lady sprang up and gave him her hand.

'The horns have shrunk a little, Doctor.'

He gave her a slice of orange. 'I shall come for my fee, Your Highness, in the morning.'

She awoke in the morning and looked in her mirror. The horns had disappeared. The King and Queen heard how the horns had been got rid of by this doctor. They gave him as much money as he could carry.

He took his money and went back to the three roads, where he was to meet his brother. It was midnight: he fell asleep under the hedge. In the morning he saw a man coming towards him.

'Who comes there?' cried he.

'It is I,' said his brother. 'So you are here before me, eh?'

'What sort of luck have you had, my boy?' asked Jack.

'I've gained naught. I'm destitute. I have lost all my money. And how did *you* reach here, being blind?'

'I have had better luck than you,' said Jack, 'I've got new eyes, and a bag of money twice as big as the one you took when you made me blind.'

That was all. Jack didn't say any more about what his brother had done.

So now the two brothers set off together to the cave to visit the old woman – the armless and legless one. They found her and rewarded her with some gold pieces. Then the two brothers went to their own little village and built a new house there. And there they live together with a little maidservant, and now they never fall out with one another.

That is all I know about those two brothers. Find out more for yourselves if ye wish!

6

The Little Crop-tailed Hen

Once upon a time there were two great big mansions. In one lived a widow and in the other a widower. The old lady had a daughter, and so had the old gentleman. The old lady's daughter was an ill-favoured creature, and a hunchback as well. As for the old gentleman's daughter, she was a beauty. The widow and the widower married. Then they all four lived together in the old gentleman's mansion.

The ugly little hunchback had to go down to the well with a pail to fetch water. She took the pail and went down. There was a cottage near the gate, and a little old witch-woman lived there. She was standing at the door, and she invited the hunchbacked girl to come in and to have something to eat.

The little hunchback was proud, and now she grew angry: 'Aren't you ashamed to ask me to enter such a wretched hovel?'

She left the old witch-woman and went down

to the well. She dipped her pail in the well. Three boars' heads arose out of the water. Said one of them:

'Lift me, and wipe me, and comb me, and set me down softly.'

Not she! She struck them down with her pail. Then she dipped the pail back in the well and she drew it up again full of muddy water. She went home.

'Why have you brought back muddy water?' asked the old lady, her mother.

'I saw nothing but muddy water in the well,' says the girl.

Now the other girl – the beautiful one – goes out with the pail to go to the well. She goes down the road and she comes to the old witch-woman's cottage. The witch-woman was standing at the door, and said to the beautiful young woman:

'Will you come in, my lady, and have a mouthful to eat?'

'Yes, I will,' and in she went. She had something to eat. The old witch-woman gave her a little sweet milk and some bread and butter.

The girl left and came out of the cottage. She went down to the well. She dipped her pail in the well. Up sprang three boars' heads. Said one to the fair young lady: 'Lift me, and wipe me, and comb me, and set me down softly.'

She lifted him, she wiped him, she combed him, and she set him down softly. She filled her pail with water. The water was clear. She went home with it. The old lady – her step-mother –. was bewildered. She didn't know what to make of it.

'How is it that you, step-daughter, can fetch clear water while you, daughter, bring back muddy water?'

On the next day, it was the hunchback girl's turn to fetch the water. She set off. She saw the old witch-woman by the door of her cottage.

'Will you come in, my lady, and have a mouthful to eat?'

But the hunchback girl was proud: 'Not I! Aren't you ashamed to ask me?'

She went to the well and dipped in her pail. Up sprang the three boars' heads.

Said the second one: 'Lift me, and wipe me, and comb me, and set me down softly.'

She did the same as before; she just struck them with the pail. She drew up a pailful of muddy water and went home. Her mother was furious to see such muddy water again.

Now here is the other girl going to fetch water. Down she goes, and she comes to the old witch-woman's cottage.

'Will you come in, my lady, and have something to eat?'

'Yes, I will.' She went in and had something to eat. She bade the little old witch-woman 'Good day', and went on down to the well. She dipped her pail in the water. Up sprang the three boars' heads.

Said one: 'Lift me, and wipe me, and comb me, and set me down softly.'

The beautiful girl did so, filled her pail with clear water, and went home. The old lady – her step-mother – was furious to see her step-daughter bringing home clear water.

'How comes it that this girl brings clear water, while my child brings muddy water?' said she to herself. 'I'll send them both tomorrow, one after the other.'

Next day came; down went the little hunchback.

The little old witch-woman was standing at her door, just as before.

'Will you come in, my lady, and have something to eat?'

'Aren't you ashamed, you old hag, to ask me to come in?' said the proud girl, and went to the well and dipped in her pail. Up sprang the three boars' heads once more.

'Lift me, wipe me, comb me, and set me down softly.'

Again, she struck down the heads with her pail.

She turned to go home and saw three fine gentlemen standing before her.

Said the eldest: 'Here is a grand lady!'

'Yes brother,' said the second. 'What do you wish for this lady?'

'I wish that one side of her head shall be all bald.'

He asked the youngest brother, 'And what do you wish for this lady?'

'I wish that the other side of her hair shall be covered with nits.'

Now the eldest brother speaks: 'She is ugly enough now; I wish that she be ten times more hideous when she gets home.'

And now the fair girl goes to fetch water. She comes to the little old witch-woman's cottage.

'Will you come in, my lady, and have a mouthful to eat?'

'Yes I will,' and in she went. She ate and came out.

She reached the well. She dipped in the pail. Up came the three boars' heads.

'Lift me, and wipe me, and comb me, and set me down softly.'

She did so. After she'd done, the heads sank down. She drew a pailful of clear water. She turned her head; she saw three young gentlemen just as her step-sister had done.

The eldest said to the others: 'Here is a lovely young lady!'

'Aye, she is a lovely lady indeed!'

'What do you wish for this young lady?'

Said one, 'I wish that one side of her hair shall be all gold. What do you wish, brother?'

'I wish that the other side shall be all silver.'

'And what is your wish, brother?' they said to the eldest.

'She is beautiful enough now; I wish that she be ten times more beautiful when she reaches home.'

And now the two step-sisters are at home. The mother was scared half out of her wits when she saw them – the one so hideous and the other so wonderfully beautiful. She couldn't bear to see either of them. It made her ill to look at them. She took to her bed and called her husband.

'What shall we do with these two?'

The old man pondered a while, and waited for his wife to speak before he uttered a word. 'I don't know what to do,' he says at last.

Said his wife: 'Make a great chest and put them both into it and cast them into the sea and let them go wherever the wind carries them.'

It was done, just as she said.

Lo! The two step-sisters are out at sea now, where they have been for a month. Their food was nearly gone. There were a few crusts left and one egg, but this last egg was one that the beautiful girl had been keeping warm in her bosom; trying to hatch it.

Hatch it did, but not into a little yellow chicken. It hatched straight away into a little crop-tailed hen. Up flew this little hen and settled into the fair lady's lap, and looked about her. She looked into the face of the fair lady, and she looked across at the ugly one. Then she spoke.

'Mammy,' said the little hen, 'who is this ugly creature with you?'

The fair one told her.

'That's my aunt then,' said the little hen.

Now they had only a few crusts. The fair lady found a small penknife in her pocket. She opened it. She had a good look at the chest, and she found where the join of the lid was. She cut a little hole with the knife and thrust her finger through the opening. She sawed away again to make the hole larger. Then she put her head through to see where they were. She saw fields. She turned back and said to the other girl: 'I have seen fields.'

The water grew shallower and shallower. The wind blew them closer to the land, and she worked away until she at last made a hole wide enough for them to creep through. They escaped, left the chest behind, and walked up an old by-lane. They found an empty barn.

The little crop-tailed hen went in to see what sort of a place it was. Back she came and told her mother:

'It's all right, there's plenty of straw and the place is dry. Come in.'

The three entered. Said the little hen to the one she called her aunt:

'Go and hide yourself in the straw.'

She did, and the little hen heaped more straw over her.

'And do you, Mammy, sit there. I am going to beg food for you.'

The little hen went up the lane. She found a great mansion. She went up to the mansion and knocked at the door. The butler came out to see who was there. He saw a little crop-tailed hen. He took no notice of her. He went in and shut the door. The little hen knocked at the door again. Out came the butler.

Said the little hen, 'I want food for my mammy.'

The butler went back to his old master and mistress. 'A little crop-tailed hen is out there, begging for food for her Mother.' The master and mistress rose and came to the door.

There was the little hen.

'I want food for my mammy.'

So in they went, collected some victuals, brought them out and fastened them upon the little hen's back.

See! Here is the little hen setting off. And now she has got to the barn.

'I have brought food for you, Mammy; give my ugly aunt something to eat and then let her hide herself again.'

That food lasted the three for three days. Now it was finished.

The little hen goes again to the great mansion. She got victuals in the same way as she got them before, and brought them home to the barn. Once more the food came to an end.

'I will find food, Mammy,' said the little hen. She went to the great mansion. The butler knew what she wanted by this time, but not where she came from. The old master and mistress agreed that they would follow her in the carriage and watch where the little crop-tailed hen went. They saw her go into the empty barn. They stopped the carriage. They sent the butler to peep through the window.

He saw a beautiful young lady with the little hen beside her, and they were eating. He told his master. His master alighted and went into the barn and spoke with the young lady. He saw

The wedding of the Young Master and the Beautiful Lady

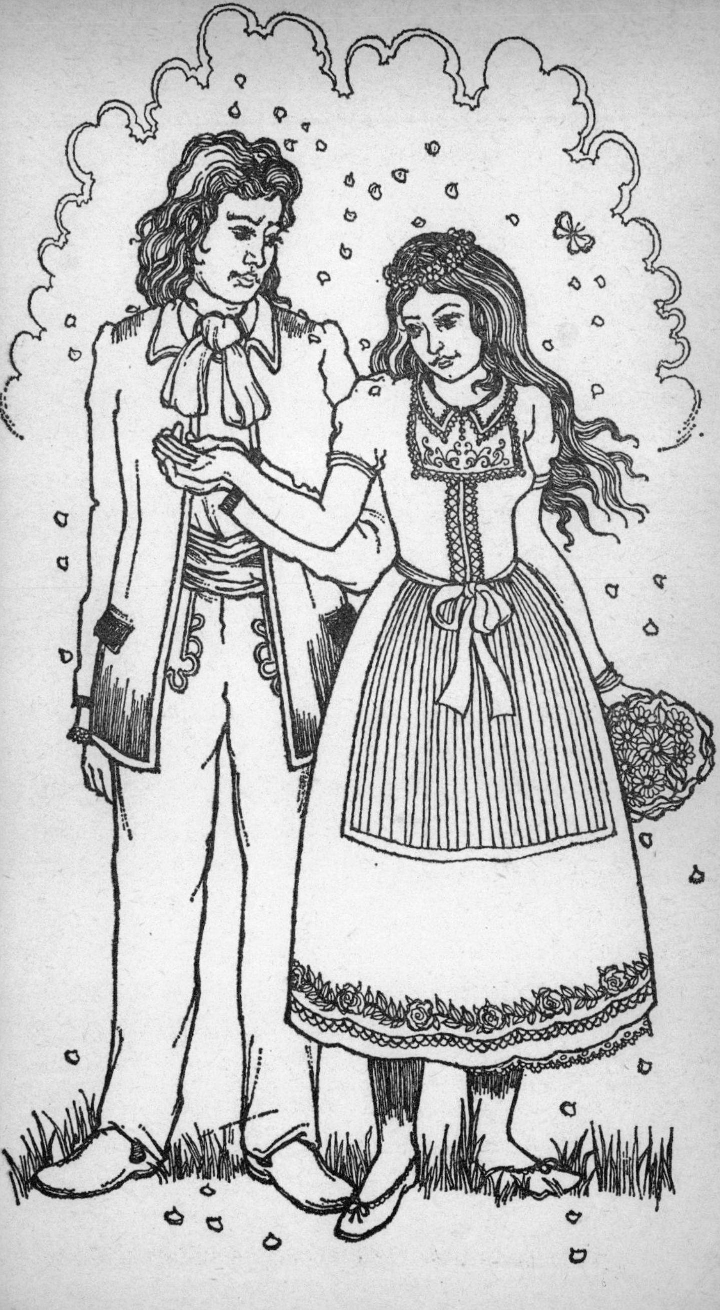

nothing of the hunchback; she was hidden in the straw. They took the lady and the little hen into the carriage and drove back to the great mansion. The young master was there. As soon as the beautiful lady entered the great hall of the mansion he gazed upon her; he loved her; he married her.

But the ugly lady was sent home.

The little crop-tailed hen stayed with her mother; no money could buy her. I was there, and at the wedding I played the fiddle for them, and they paid me handsomely.

That's all I have to tell.

7

Twopence Halfpenny

There were three brothers, and the three were travelling along the road looking for work. Night came upon them and they didn't know where to go to find a lodging. It was dark and the road they were on led through a forest.

At last they saw a glimmer of light, and they came to a cottage. The door stood open. They saw a table with supper spread upon it.

'Go in,' said the eldest brother.

'No, I won't,' said the second. 'Go in yourself.'

'Not I, in faith!'

'You're fools, the pair of you,' said the youngest. And in he went, and sat down at the table and ate his fill. The other two watched him. They were afraid to go into the house. But at last they too went in and sat down and ate.

Lo and behold! A little old woman appears.

'I have seen no man here for years,' says she. 'Where do you come from?'

'We are looking for work.'

'I'll find work for you tomorrow.'

They went to bed. In the morning they got up early, and on the fire was a great pot of porridge and milk. And that was what they ate.

And now the old woman tells the eldest brother to fetch the tools from the barn, and to go to the forest to fell trees. He takes off his coat, and here he is, working hard! There came a voice that asked him who had told him to fell the forest trees? He couldn't see who spoke because it was a little dwarf. Then he looked under his feet and saw him in the grass. (He was a tiny little mannikin, you must know – no bigger than twopence halfpenny.)

But he was strong! The little man struck the eldest brother, beat him until he bled and left him there.

Now the serving girl came out with his dinner. She saw him on the ground and she went back and told the other two brothers to come and fetch him. They brought him back and put him to bed.

In the morning the second brother went to the forest. The eldest brother told him it was a tiny little dwarf who had thrashed him. The second brother laughed at him.

And now he too sets off for the forest. He takes off his coat and starts felling. Lo! There is something asking him who bade him cut down the trees? Well!

He looked all round him; he could see nothing. And it was a long time before he caught sight of the dwarf. Then he saw him in the grass.

'Begone!' said the young man, but the little stranger beat him to a jelly. The girl came with dinner as before and went back and told the two brothers to come and carry him home. They went down to the forest and brought him home.

The youngest brother laughed at them both.

'Tomorrow I'll go down,' says he.

In the morning he goes down to the forest. And here he is felling trees! He hears something. He looks and sees the little dwarf in the grass. The lad gave him a kick.

'You had best keep quiet,' said the dwarf, and struck him.

Down fell the lad, and the little old dwarf well-nigh murdered him.

He was lying there when the girl came with his dinner. Back she went and she told the other two brothers to come and fetch him. The two went.

'No,' said the youngest one, 'leave me here and go away.' The two brothers went home.

The youngest lay there and watched. What he

saw was that the little old man crept away under a big stone.

When the dwarf had gone, the lad went home and he and his brothers went to the stables and brought the horses out – all four of them. They took a stout rope and the three young men went down to the forest with the four horses and fastened the rope round the stone. They made the horses drag it away and underneath they found a well.

'Go down, you!' said the eldest brother.

'Not I!' said the second.

'I'll go,' says the youngest. 'Make the rope fast and let me down. When you hear me say "Pull up", pull me up, and when I say "Let me down", let me down.'

The two elder brothers made the rope fast and let him down.

He came to a beautiful country and saw the old dwarf. This time the little old man talked with him in a friendly way.

'Since you've come into this land, I'll tell you something. You'll find three castles. In the first lives a giant with two heads. You must fight with him. Choose the rusty sword. I'll be there.'

'I shall be afraid of him!'

'Go forward and have no fear. I shall be there with you.'

And now here is the lad knocking at the castle door.

A serving maid came to him and he asked where the master was.

'He is in the castle. Do you wish to see him?'

'Yes,' said Jack, 'I want to fight with him.'

'He will kill you!'

'Go and tell him to come out.'

The girl went and told the giant to come out.

'Do you want something to eat?' asked the giant.

'No,' says the lad. 'Come out and I'll fight with you.'

'Come here then and choose a sword!'

The lad chose the rusty old sword.

'Why do you choose that rusty old sword? Take a bright one!'

'Not I! This one will do for me.'

The two take their stand before the door. Off went one head.

'Spare my life and I'll give you all my money!'

'No.' The lad struck off the other head. He killed the giant.

This was the Copper Castle – so men called it.

And now the lad goes to the next – the Silver Castle. A giant with three heads lived there. The

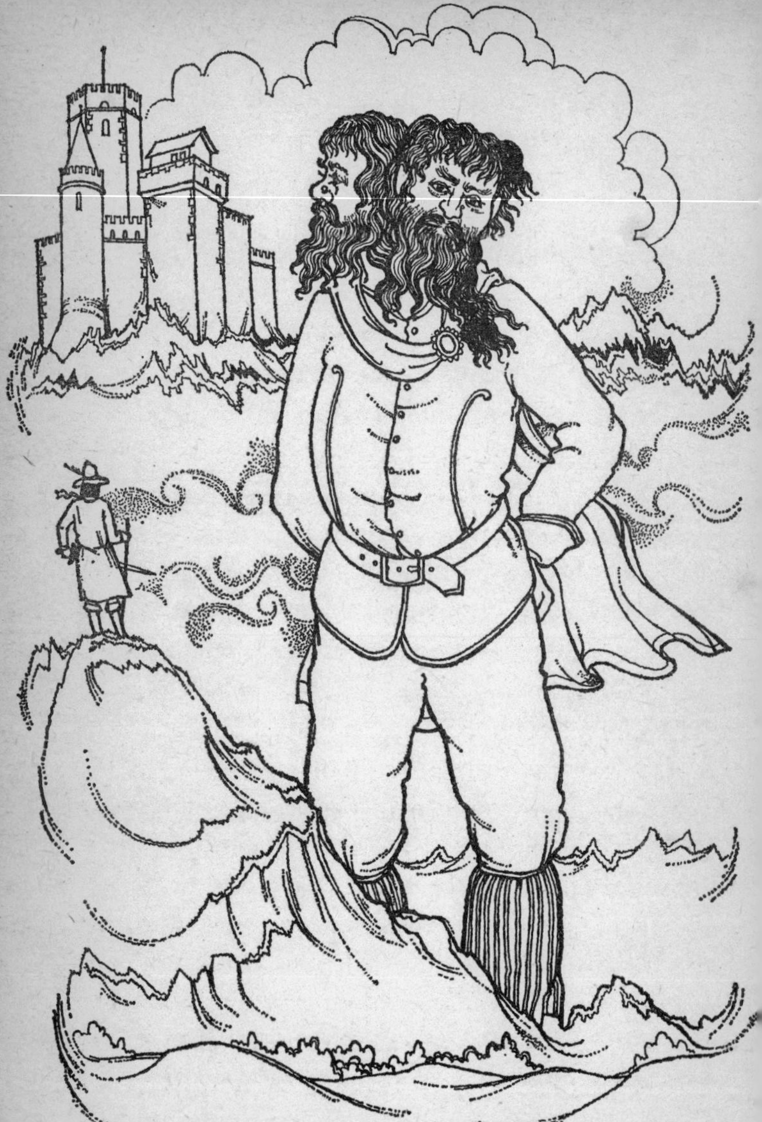

lad took the rusty sword and struck off two heads.

'Don't kill me; spare my life and I'll give you the keys of the castle!'

'Not I,' was the answer, and off went the third head.

And now the lad goes to the last – to the Golden Castle. The giant who lived there had four heads.

'Have you come here to fight with me?'

'Yes.'

They went out, and with the rusty old sword the lad struck off three heads.

'Don't kill me and I'll give you my castle!'

'Yes, I will,' – and off went the last head.

Now all the castles and all the money and the three fair ladies that were shut up in the three castles were his. So off he sets, and the lady from the Golden Castle with him. He went back to the Silver Castle and fetched that lady. Then he went to the Copper Castle and got that lady. And the four went on and came to the spot where the lad had climbed down.

The old dwarf was waiting there for him, but not so friendly this time. The lad – the youngest brother – sent the three ladies up to the top where his two brothers were waiting. But now the two wouldn't pull their younger brother up, and

Out came the Giant with Two Heads

though the dwarf was there he wanted meat before he would help. For that the youngest brother went back to the Copper Castle. He cooked some meat for him, and after that the old dwarf sent him up a little way. Then he stopped: again he wanted meat. The lad had some left, so he gave him some. The dwarf sent him up a little higher. He stopped; he wanted meat. Again the lad gave him some. He went a little higher still. 'Give me some meat.' There was none left. The lad didn't know what to do. So he felt in his pocket and pulled out his knife, and cut a little flesh from his leg, and gave it to the old dwarf.

So, at last, the youngest brother reached the top. But his two brothers had gone off with two of the ladies, and had left the third one behind. The eldest brother had taken the Golden lady and the second brother had taken the Silver lady, and they had left the Copper lady for the one that had freed them all. He asked her where they had gone. The lady told him and he hurried after them. He overtook them by the church – they were going to be married.

The fairest lady – the Golden one – looked back at the youngest brother.

'That girl shall be mine,' said he, and sure enough, he managed to get her away from his brother and married her. He left the Silver lady for the eldest brother to marry. There was only the second brother now, and he took the Copper lady.

So here are all three brothers and all three ladies.

And now they want to go down to the three castles.

The youngest brother spoke to the tiny little old dwarf about taking them down.

'I will take you all down, but you must give me food on the way.'

'All right,' they said. 'We will give you plenty of food.'

'Then I will take you down.'

And down he carried them all.

So one brother and one lady went to live in the Copper Castle, and the other brother and his lady in the Silver Castle. And the youngest brother and his lady went to the Golden Castle. And he kept the little old dwarf for the rest of his life.

There now! I've done!

8

Appy Boswell's Monkey

Appy had a monkey, which he'd kept for ten years, and fed on the best of everything and done well by in every way. Now this monkey it would never once talk with him, nor answer his questions, nor even as much as say thank you when he gave it its vittles.

One day when Appy had sat himself down by the side of a brick kiln, the monkey being with him, a thought came into his head about it refusing to speak with him.

'Well,' he says to himself, 'come what will, I'll make the beggar talk.' So he goes over to the kiln, an' there he finds an empty brick oven – scorching hot! Now what does he do but he takes the monkey, and he puts it inside this oven, an' claps a sheet of iron over the mouth of it so that the monkey can't get out.

After about ten minutes of this the monkey began squealing.

'No mortal man could stand this,' it calls out

to Appy, 'so for why should you expect me to? Release me or I shall die!' At this Appy opens the door.

'Will you promise me that you'll talk with me for the future?' he asks it, 'and answer all my questions?'

'Yes, I'll promise,' the monkey answers, and so Appy lets it out again.

So, when Appy got home that night he says to his wife: 'Anis,' he says, 'the monkey spoke well with me today, and so now,' he says, 'I'm going to give him a treat.' He goes and makes him a big bowl of eatables – the best that he had – and sets this before his monkey. Then, after it has eaten its fill, he asks it, 'Have you enjoyed your vittles?'

But it doesn't answer him not a word; it only nods its head.

Then he asks it: 'Have you had a bellyful?' but again it won't answer him not a word.

'Oh! Very well then,' says Appy. 'You won't answer me, won't you? Then I shall take you back to that hot place again.'

Now the monkey, as soon as ever it hears this, it comes forward and it puts out its hand, an' it strokes Appy on his cheek.

'I'll answer you anything,' it says, 'if only you'll not take me back there again.'

9

The Maid of The Mill

There was a big mill and an old miller and his wife and their daughter. The daughter was beautiful. The old people did not want her to marry yet. They wanted her to stay with them a while longer and not make a match of it with any of the young men who came to the mill to buy flour.

One day the old folks went off to have a day's pleasuring together. The girl was left alone. A young man came, that she didn't know very well, and had a talk with her.

'I have five barrels outside. Will they be in your way if I leave them there for the night?' he asked.

'No, they won't be in my way at all.'

Two or three more words passed between them and then he took himself off.

Now night fell. The girl went upstairs. A suspicion crossed her mind about the man who brought the barrels.

She looked through the window and she saw two strange men crawling out of two of the barrels. She thought that they looked like robbers. She locked herself in; she took her father's sword in her hand. There was a little window on to the landing in the inner wall of her room. The first man came upstairs.

'Where are you?' cried he.

'Here I am. Put your head through here.' He thrust his head through the small window. She struck off his head with the sword.

He had a silver whistle round his neck. It fell down at the girl's feet. She picked it up and blew it. The other robbers heard the signal. Up came another.

'Where are you?'

'Here I am. Put your head through here.' She struck off his head with the sword.

She blew the whistle again. Up came another. She slew him. Up came the other two robbers, one by one. She slew them with the sword as she had slain their three brothers.

Behold! Five heads inside the room, and five dead robbers outside!

She blew the silver whistle again. Lo! Another robber comes up. This one was the eldest brother. He thought that all his brethren were inside plundering the house.

'Where are you?'

'Here I am. Put your head through here.' He did so. She struck at his head with the sword. She wounded him but did not kill him. Then he knew that his brothers had been slain. He was terrified and fled home.

Now morning broke. The two old people returned home. They were shocked to see what had taken place in the house.

'How did all this happen, daughter?'

'Have patience, Mother, and I will tell you.' So she told them. 'Robbers came here to the house. I went upstairs and locked myself into my own room with my father's sword in my hand. As they put their heads through the little window I slew them, one by one.'

Now I will pass on to the house of the robbers. Here is the eldest robber at home. He tells his mother about the miller's daughter. The old woman was furious to hear that her five sons had been killed. But they could not think how to get hold of the young woman.

'I will tell you what you must do,' said the Mother. 'Disguise yourself with a false beard, and dress yourself in your best clothes, and pretend to be a grand gentleman that comes there to buy flour. Beware of taking off your hat, or she will see where she wounded you. Pretend to woo the young woman; use sweet words and bring her here.'

The robber's head was healed now. He had a silver plate to hide the wound made by the sword. He dressed himself in lordly apparel, put on a false beard, and went down to the mill.

Through the window the girl saw him coming up to the house. She ran to her father.

'Here comes a gentleman, Father.'

'Who is he?' asked her father.

'I don't know,' said the girl.

The old miller came down to him. He gave him his hand. 'How are you, sir? Step in.'

He came in, and seated himself. He talked to the girl in a lover-like way. The girl lost her heart to him. He went home and told his mother.

'I will soon bring her here, Mother.'

Down to the mill he went again. The girl saw him. She went out and gave him her hand. She was in love with him. The girl led him inside. The pair sat down and had a chat.

'Would you like to visit my home?'

'Yes, I should,' said she. The girl went upstairs and dressed herself, and set out with him.

Now the two have reached the robbers' house.

'Ah ha! I see you've got her, boy!'

'I have got her. Aye! I have got her!'

He took off his hat and the young woman caught sight of his head.

'Ah!' murmured the girl. 'It is the Robber Chief.' And she was sore afraid; she didn't know where she was.

So they put the girl under lock and key. Then the mother and son discussed what should be done with her. 'Do you know the old cauldron in the outhouse, Mother?' said the son.

'Yes,' said the old woman.

'Make her bring the cauldron full of water and kindle a fire under it. We will boil her in the cauldron. Strip her ready, old woman, I will be there anon.'

The old hag went and unlocked the door.

'Come here, young woman, I want you. You see that cauldron over there?'

'Yes,' said the young woman.

'Go and bring it full of water.' She brought it full of water.

'Kindle a fire under it.' She kindled a fire under it.

'That water is for you to be boiled in. Strip off your clothes and give them to me. My son will be here presently.'

The old hag took away her clothes and locked the door on her, leaving her naked.

The young woman didn't know what to do:

she looked around her. She saw a tiny crack in the wall – the house was an old mud hovel. She seized an old poker. She went up to the mud wall and hammered at it with the poker. She made a hole that she could creep through and she escaped.

Now the son came home.

'Where is the young woman, Mother?'

'There she is, locked up.' The son went and opened the door. He saw no one there. He went to his mother.

'Devil take you, Mother! Why couldn't you look after her?'

He called out his men. 'The young woman has escaped, comrades, let us go in search of her.' They took swords and guns and gave chase. The girl heard them coming. She climbed into an oak-tree to hide herself. The robbers halted under the very same tree.

It is getting dark now.

'Here is an oak, perhaps she is hiding in it,' said the Robber Chief.

He thrust his sword among the branches, and pricked her bare foot with it. A drop or two of blood fell upon his face.

'Let us go home, my men, it is going to rain. It is growing too dark now, we will find her early in the morning.' They went home.

The young woman climbed down and hurried off. She crossed the hills, and towards dawn she struck the high road. She saw a cart coming. She was ashamed to show herself; she hid among the bracken. The cart came nearer. She raised her head and looked at the man. He was an old servant of her father's. She hailed him. The man pulled up, and stared at her. He recognized her.

'In the name of God, how did you come here?' he asked.

'I will tell you another time; take me home, the Robber Chief is hunting me. What have you got in the cart?'

'Cases full of apples.'

'Hide me somewhere.'

'I have no hiding place, young lady, unless I put you in one of the cases underneath the apples.'

'If you meet a man on horseback who asks about me, say that you haven't seen any naked woman.'

The man emptied a case, put her inside, and covered her over with apples. He whipped up his horse and they went on. Presently he espied a horseman far off.

'I see a man on horseback, young lady.'

'Say nothing.'

The Robber Chief came up to the cart.

'Where have you come from?' he asked.

She raised her hand and hailed the carter

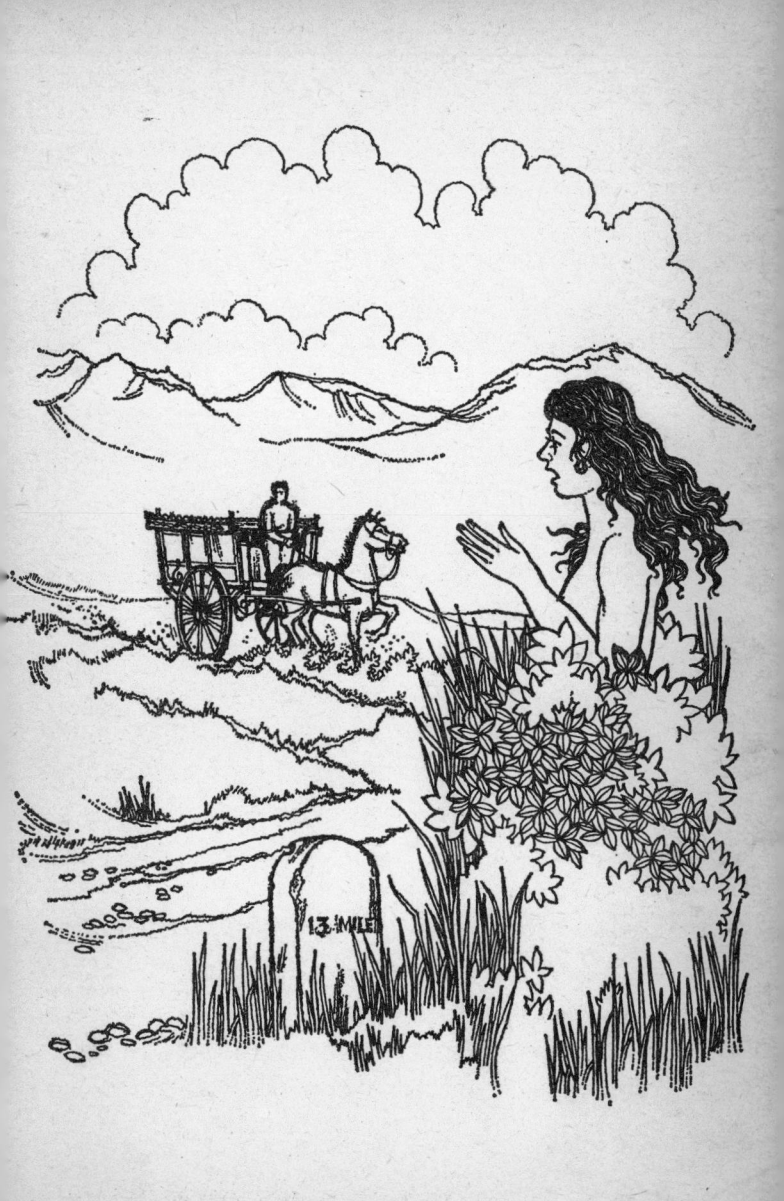
13 MILE

'I had to fetch apples from such and such a place.'

'Have you seen a young woman, naked, upon the road?'

'No, I have seen nothing.'

'I will search your cart.'

'Search it if you wish.'

The Robber Chief leapt down and went to the cart.

There were three cases of apples in it. The driver was sitting on the case in which the girl was hiding. The Robber opened one case. He found nothing but apples. He opened another. Still apples. He muttered to himself: 'Nothing but apples there.' He rode off to seek her elsewhere.

'The Robber Chief has gone, young lady.' said the carter.

The Robber Chief rode a great distance in search of her. He scoured the country for miles and miles, and at last caught the cart up again close to her home. It occurred to him that he had not searched the last case. He stopped the cart once more. The old man was sitting on the case.

'Get up, I want to see what is inside.'

'There is nothing but apples,' said the carter. He got up angrily and opened it. The Robber turned over a few apples.

'Don't bruise all my apples, I want to sell them.'

'No, she is not here,' muttered the Chief. He mounted his horse and rode off.

'The Robber Chief has gone away again, young lady,' said the carter. 'Have no fear, he won't come back.' He whipped up his horse.

Presently they reached home. The man went into the house. He told the old lady that he had seen a naked woman by the high road, hidden among the bracken.

'Where is she?' said the old lady.

'I have her in the cart; I hid her beneath the apples.'

'Here, take this blanket, wrap it round her and bring her in.'

The old lady looked at her.

'It is my child.' She was carried upstairs and put to bed. The old lady questioned the man as to how it had come about. The carter told her all he knew. She thanked him again and again. There was nothing in the house good enough for the old lady to give him.

The old folks did not know what steps to take to catch the Robber Chief.

'I will tell you, wife,' said the old man at last, 'I will tell you what must be done. Send hither and thither throughout the land to tell everyone that a banquet will be held here, followed by a ball.'

The feast is prepared and all the young men in the neighbourhood have assembled. But the Robber Chief was afraid to come. The young woman came into the room to see whether he was there. She told her father that he was not there.

'Have patience, daughter, we will go to fetch the one who is absent.'

The old man, with three or four men, went in a trap to fetch him. They reached the robber's house and the miller went in. His men waited outside. The robber stood up and shook hands with the old man.

'Are you coming down to the mill?'

'No, I am not in the mood to come. I am not well.'

'Come down, we will take you; my trap is at the door.'

He needed much persuasion before he would come. At last, he put on his hat and went with them. He arrived at the house and entered the room. The Robber Chief kept his hat on his head. All the gentlemen asked him: 'Why don't you take off your hat?'

'I never take off my hat.'

Now they are all feasting. Everyone had to make

a speech after the feast was over. The young woman entered after all had had their say. Now it is the young woman's turn to speak. The whole table is listening.

'There was a young man who used sometimes to come here to buy flour. Once he came in the afternoon with five barrels. He left them under my window. Neither my father nor my mother was at home. I was alone. His five brothers were hiding in those barrels. Night fell. They crept out to rob the house. The five brothers thrust their heads through my small window. I had my father's sword and I struck off their heads one after another ... The eldest brother put his head through last of all. I wounded him on the head but did not kill him.'

The Robber Chief sat there. He was trembling with fear. He said not a word. The girl went on:

'He came here again, disguised – finely dressed. He made love to me. I did not recognize him; I went with him to visit his mother. They made ready to boil me. The old woman forced me to strip off my clothes and left me locked up in a room. The house was built of mud. I broke a way out with a poker and fled, naked. The robbers hunted me.' The Robber Chief sat and trembled, and the girl went on to tell about hiding naked in the bracken, and about seeing the cart, and how the Robber had searched it twice.

At last the girl pointed a finger at him where he sat, and said: 'Behold the Robber Chief here, in front of you! If you don't all believe me, pull off his hat. You will find for yourselves a silver plate upon his head where I wounded him with my father's sword!'

He never left the mill alive!

10

Goggle-eyes

There lived an old widow. She had three sons, and they lived in a little hut on the mountains. On a day when a storm was raging outside and there was deep snow, the old woman wanted a few sticks to make a good fire to bake her cakes. Only one little stick was left to put on the fire.

'Go, one of you, and get me a few sticks,' she said to her sons. She begged and she begged; not one moved.

At last the eldest son got up. He opened the door. He saw the snow and turned in again and shut the door. But after a lot more persuasion he went. Lo! Here he is now, in the forest. He gathers a few sticks here and a few there, until he has made up a small faggot.

He walked on and saw a lofty watch-tower among the trees. Never before in his life had he set eyes on it. He crept around it to find out whether it had a door: it had no door. He saw one little window high up. Lo! A huge head looks out. It has great big eyes!

'Hi! Young man, do something for an old gentleman? Fetch me some water in that little pitcher by that spring over there.'

'What will you give me, Goggle-eyes?'

'Alas, I've nothing to give you. I'm very poor.'

'Then go and get it yourself, Goggle-eyes.'

The lad went back to pick up his faggot. Up leapt the sticks and drubbed him soundly. He fled home to his mother. He told her there were some cruel game-keepers in the wood.

'They beat me, Mother, and wouldn't let me bring home a few sticks.' He took off his shoes and sat by the fire.

Now the old woman asks the second son to get her some wood. After much persuasion he goes. He came to the forest. He gathered a few sticks here and there, until he came to this lofty watchtower. Lo! A huge head with great big eyes looks out of the window.

'Hi! Young man, do something for an old gentleman? Bring me a little water in that pitcher by that spring over there.'

'What will you give me, Goggle-eyes?' said the second brother.

'I have nothing to give you, I'm a poor man.'

'Then go and get it yourself, Goggle-eyes.'

As it happened to his brother, so it happened to him. The sticks beat him and he ran home to his mother.

Now the youngest brother – Will – was a simpleton who sat in the ashes by the hearth. He got up and shook himself: he shook pounds of ashes from his coat. And he fell a-laughing at his two brothers.

'It is my turn now,' says he.

He goes into the wood to gather sticks, and walks on until he comes to the lofty tower with the little window high up. Out pops the huge head again.

'Hi! Young man! Please fetch an old gentleman a little water in that pitcher by that spring over there.'

Will goes off and fetches him a pitcher of water. The old gentleman lowered a rope to him through the window. He told Will to fasten the pitcher to the rope. Will did so, and the old gentleman drew it up through the window. Now as he was doing this Will happened to be looking the other way, and, when he looked round again, there was no tower to be seen.

He heard a voice behind him: 'Will! Will!'

He looked about him but saw no one. Then he looked down at his feet, and there was a tiny dwarf hidden in the snowy grass.

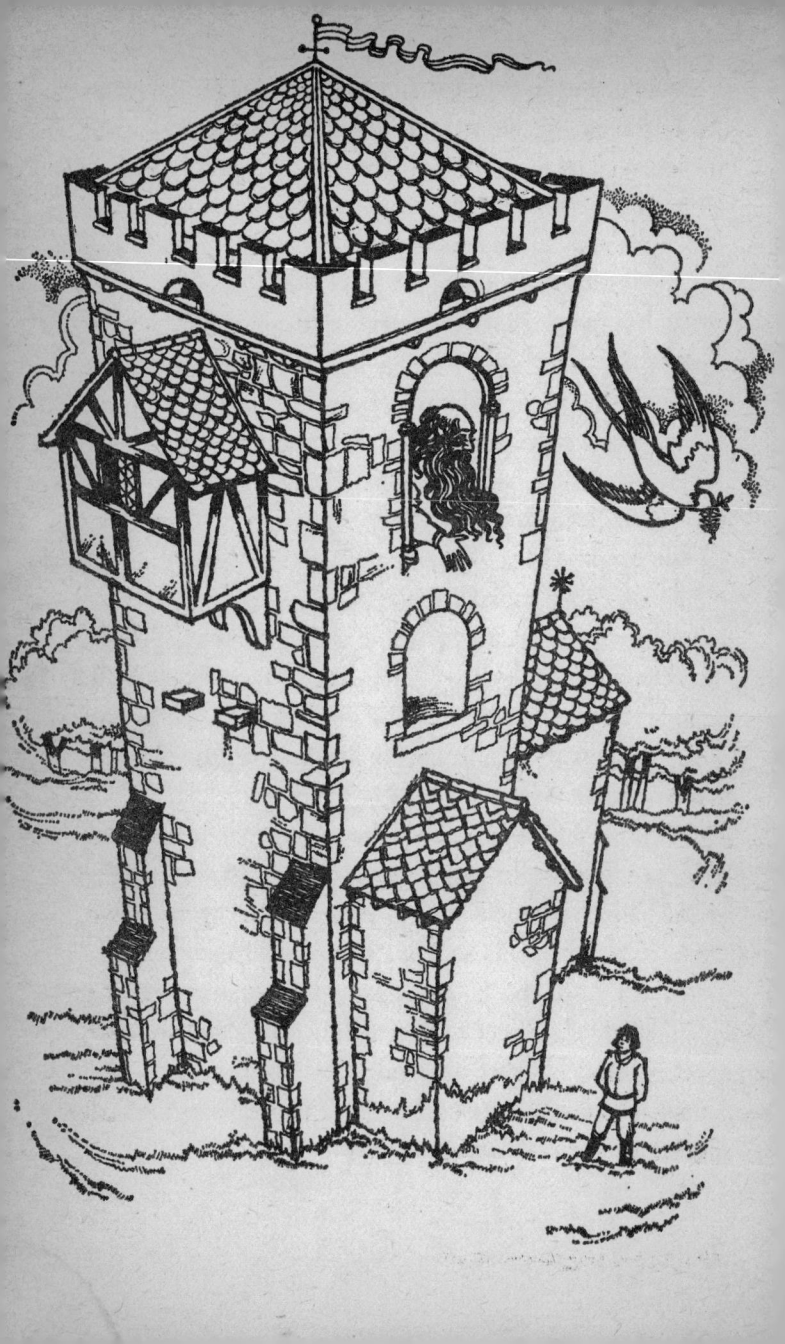

'I'm the King of the Forest, Will. You've broken my enchantment and set me free.' The little man felt in his pocket and gave Will a ring.

'Whatever you want, rub the ring, and you shall have your wish.'

Will thanked him, put the ring in his pocket and went to look for the sticks. Lo! there were the sticks all gathered together as he had left them, and he took them home to his mother.

'This will make a good blaze,' said the old woman, and she put them on the fire to bake her cakes. Will settled down by the fire again. But he still had the ring in his pocket.

Now there was a great castle nearby, and in this castle lived a young lady. Near the castle was a deep cave and at the far end of it a bag of gold; but at its entrance there burned a fierce great fire.

It was proclaimed throughout the land that the lord of the castle would give his youngest daughter to the man who could bring out the bag of gold.

All the youths of the countryside came to the spot, but the fire in the front part of the cave vanquished every one of them.

Said the eldest brother to his mother, 'I am going to win the young lady, Mother.'

Out popped Goggle-eyes again

'Bless me, boy, don't talk so foolishly!'

So the eldest boy sets off, but he couldn't get past that terrible fire in the front part of the cave, so back he came home.

And now the second brother ventures; but the fire beat him too, and home he came.

'Well,' said Will, 'now it's my turn to go, Mother.'

The old woman laughed; 'Don't be so foolish.'

But Will sets off, and he comes to the cave where the great fire was. There was a crowd about the place, but no one took any notice of Will, because everyone knew he was a fool. Will pulled out the ring and rubbed it. And Lo! after that, he could go through the fire, straight up to the bag of gold, and so he brought it out. The old lord of the castle was watching. When he saw Will pass unscathed through the fire, he said to himself, 'So he has met my brother, has he?' Then all the people went away and the lord summoned his daughters.

He asked them who the beggarman was who had got the gold, because he had just walked off home with it. None of them knew. The lord wanted very much to find out who this man could be. He sent his servants to ask at all the cottages on the mountain side. They could learn nothing about this man and they went back to the castle.

Will had brought the bag of gold home to his mother, and he'd flung it into the corner as if it were a sack of potatoes. He didn't know what gold was; he was so simple that his two brothers laughed at him. Will just rubbed the ring and wished that his poor mother should have plenty to eat, so now they all got everything they called for.

The lord of the castle was troubled. He searched every day for the man who had got through the fire. And one day when he was out driving with his lady in the carriage, he saw a cottage in the midst of the mountains that he had never noticed before. He drove home and, on the next day, sent one of his serving men to find out who lived in this cottage on the mountain side.

The serving man arrived at the hut and knocked. And the old woman came to the door.

'Who lives here?' asked the man.

'Myself and my three sons, and no one else,' she answered.

The old woman was afraid of him. She was afraid that he had come there to turn them out of the house. The servant asked to see the boys.

'Yes, sir, I will call them at once.'

She turned to the three boys and said: 'There is a gentleman at the door who wishes to see the three of you.'

The three brothers came to the door. The serving man recognized Will as soon as he saw him. He asked him a few questions, put his hand in his pocket, and gave Will five shillings. The servant went home, and told his master that he had found the man. The lord sent the carriage and the servant to bring back Will to the castle.

When Will saw the carriage he laughed aloud.

'What do you want with me?' said he, and he laughed again.

'You must get into the carriage. My lord wishes to see you at the castle.'

Will got into the carriage, and they drove off at full speed. The lord of the castle recognized him as soon as he saw him. The two elder daughters laughed at poor Will and made fun of him. But their father paid no attention to them, and ordered the butler to bring Will a tankard of ale. The lord put a few questions to him, and all the time Will's hand was in his pocket rubbing the ring.

'Where do you live, Will?' asked the lord.

'I live on the mountain side, my lord, with my two brothers and my mother.' The youngest sister kept throwing glances at Will. Said Will to himself: 'I should like that young lady to come for a walk with me.'

After they had all talked together for some time, Will said, 'I must go home to my mother now.'

The youngest sister arose and said to him, 'I will show you a short cut to your house.' They talked to each other on the way.

'What work do you do, Will?'

Will laughed. 'I do nothing except gather a few sticks for my mother.'

She showed him a footpath. 'And now I must leave you,' said she.

Will came home. 'A lovely lady, Mother, came to put me on the road from the castle.'

'You? My poor boy! Have nothing to do with a great lady like her.'

'Indeed, Mother, I will have something to do with her, and I will bring her here into the bargain.' He remembered the ring, pulled it out of his pocket and rubbed it. 'I should like to see the King of the Forest.'

As soon as the word was spoken, someone tapped him on the shoulder.

'Here I am, Will; what do you want?' It was Goggle-eyes.

'I should like to marry the youngest lady – the daughter of the lord of the castle.'

'Very well, Will,' said he. 'What else do you want?'

'I should like a large mansion near your tower in the forest.'

As soon as the word was spoken, there was the mansion in the forest. He rubbed the ring again and wished the young lady to drive up the hill in a carriage. As soon as he had uttered the wish he saw the carriage and pair coming, with the lady inside and two coachmen on the box. They drew up when they saw Will and stood still. The young lady stepped out of the carriage and held out her hand to Will. Will took her to his own mansion and they were married.

They lived happily from that day to this, and Will became game-keeper to his father-in-law. And he left the bag of gold behind for his mother and his brothers.

I got a big pudding for telling this lie!

11

The Green Man of No Man's Land

There was a mill, a young man, and his maidservant. Now this young man was a great gambler. No one could beat him: he beat everybody.

There came a gentleman to him. He was dressed from top to toe in green and this man in green walked straight into the miller's room. The two had a pleasant word together.

'Will you play me at cards?' asked the gentleman in green of the young miller. The cards were on the table.

'Yes,' said the miller.

Now the two are at their game. The miller beat the gentleman. The gentleman asked the young miller, 'What will you have for your win?'

'I'll have a castle yonder.' As soon as he said the word there was a castle.

The gentleman said: 'Will you have another game?'

'Yes.'

And now the two are at their game, and this time the gentleman in green beat the miller.

And the gentleman said: 'This time you must find my castle. My name is "The Green Man of No Man's Land". And if you don't find my castle in a year and a day, I'll cut off your head.' Time passed.

And here is the young miller, setting off on horseback to look for the green man. He travelled a long, long way, and there was frost and deep snow. Night came upon him. He was hungry. He saw a little house near the road, and he got off his horse and went to the door.

He knocked. A little old woman comes out to him. The young fellow asked for a bed.

'All right!' said the old woman. 'Come in.'

He sat down by the fire. The old woman and he had a talk together. The old woman got supper ready for him. He asked the old woman whether she knew a man called 'The Green Man of No Man's Land'.

'No,' said the old woman. 'Never have I heard the name. I will let you know in the morning whether a quarter of the whole world knows.'

In the morning they had breakfast. The old woman goes outside and calls the young fellow to her. A ladder is standing by the door. The old woman climbs up on to the roof and blows a horn. Folk come hurrying up. She asked them whether they knew or had heard of 'The Green Man who lives in No Man's Land'. No, said the folk, they had never heard the name. All the people went away.

The old woman blew again. The birds come flying to her now. She asked the birds the same question: did they know of 'The Green Man who lives in No Man's Land'? They had never heard the name.

'Then begone.' They flew away.

The old woman came down. She said to the young miller, 'Further on I have a sister. Go there; she will speak more wisely to you. She knows more than I know. Take my horse and leave yours here.'

She gave him a ball of thread, and told him to throw the ball forward, over the horse's ears. The way the thread led him was the way he must go. He set off, and he threw the ball of thread as she had said. He came to the house just as the old woman had told him. The second old woman spoke to him,

'It is a long time,' said she, 'since I have seen my sister's horse.' He put the horse in the stable. The old woman called him into the house to have supper. The two sat down to table and ate; they finished eating. The young fellow asked again whether she had heard of 'The Green Man who lives in No Man's Land'.

'No,' said the old woman, 'never have I heard such a name. In the morning I will tell you whether half the world knows it.' They went to their beds.

In the morning they dressed themselves. The two came down and ate their breakfast. Then the old woman went outside. She called the young miller to her. The old woman climbed up a ladder and blew a horn, just as her sister had done. Lo! Half the people in the world come hurrying up to her. Then the old woman speaks the name – 'The Green Man who Lives in No Man's Land'. No, they had never heard the name.

'Then begone!' The old woman blew the horn again. Lo! Half the birds in the world come flying to her. She asks them whether they knew or had heard of the name. No, they had never heard it.

'Then begone!'

'I have a sister,' said the old woman, 'and if she knows not, then there is none who knows. Take my horse, young man, and leave my sister's horse here. Take a ball of thread and throw it in front of you over the horse's ears. Follow as it unwinds.' He did so.

Now he comes to the house, and here is the oldest sister at the door. She stares at him as he rides up.

'That is my sister's horse, I have not seen him for a great while. Put the horse in the stable, and give him some food.'

He did so. The old woman called him into the house to have some supper. The two sat down to table. They ate and finished eating. He talked to the old woman and asked whether she knew the name of such a man. 'No,' said the old woman, 'I have never heard it. I will let you know in the morning.' Then they went to their beds.

In the morning the old woman did as her sisters had done. She got up, made a fire, put the kettle on, and called him to come downstairs. He did so. He comes to the table to have his breakfast. They finish. He and the old woman sit by the fire, and he smokes his pipe. He has a talk with the old woman and she gets up and goes outside. This old woman also climbs up a ladder and blows a horn. Lo! This time it is all the people in the world who come hurrying up to her. The old woman speaks the name to them – 'The Green Man who Lives in No Man's Land'. No, they had never heard the name.

'Begone,' said the old woman. The folk departed.

'Wait a little! I will call all the birds that are in the world.' The old woman blew the horn again. Lo! All the birds come flying to her. She asked them whether they knew where such a man was.

'I will tell you his name – "The Green Man of No Man's Land".'

All the birds said that no, they had never heard the name.

The old woman comes down and opens her book to see whether all the birds had been there. She found from her book that there had been one bird missing. The old woman goes back to the roof of the house and blows the horn again. Lo! the missing bird appears. It is the eagle. She says to him: 'Wretch! Where have you been all this long while?'

'I have come from the country of "The Green Man of No Man's Land",' said the eagle and then he told her where it was.

'Begone! That is all I want to know.'

'Come in, young fellow, that I may tell you. Leave my sister's horse here, and take my horse; and take a ball of thread and throw it forward over the horse's ears for a guide.' He mounted the horse. And the old woman said to him:

'Touch nothing! Let the horse go where it will. You'll see a great lake, and on the lake three

All the birds in the world came flying to her

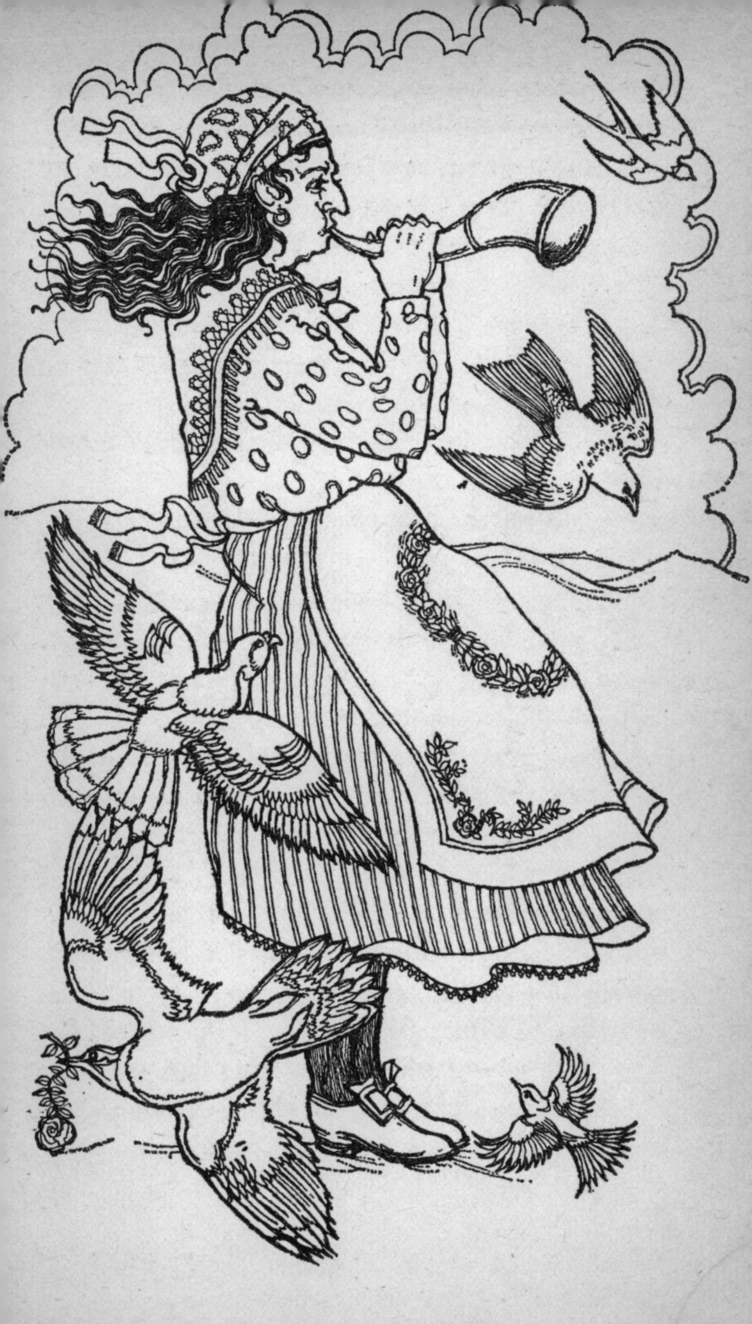

white swans; dismount and hide by the lake. These three white birds will come near you and shake down their feathers and go to bathe. Arise then, young fellow; go, take the feathers of the third and keep them safe. The third will come and beg for her feathers. Don't give them up. Tell her to carry you over the lake to her father's castle.'

The young miller set off and he found the lake just where the old woman had said. When the last swan went to the lake, he stole her feathers. She begged for them back.

'First carry me over the lake to your father's castle.'

'No,' said she, 'I have no father.'

'Yes,' said he.

'No,' said she again.

Lo! She weeps; she wants her feathers back from him!

'Carry me over the lake and you shall have your feathers.'

She agrees at last: 'But don't tell my father, when you go up to the castle, that it was I that carried you over the lake.'

She carried him over.

Now this young miller goes up to the castle. He goes to the door and knocks. Lo! The lord comes out. The young fellow saw that he was all dressed in green from top to toe and was the very gentleman he had played cards with at the mill.

'Hast found my house, young miller? Then one of my daughters has been with thee.'

'Say not so, I have not seen one of them,' said the young fellow.

'Come in.' The Green Man of No Man's Land gave him food. Then he told him to clean out the stable; 'If you don't perform this task, your head shall be cut off.'

The young fellow pulled off his coat to do the work. But for one spadeful of filth that he threw out, three came in. He grew tired. He threw the spade down – flung the thing away – and sat down. He was weary. Presently the lady came to him – the youngest lady, the one whose feathers he had stolen. She brought food. 'Get up and eat.' He got up and ate. While he was eating the stable was cleansed: all the filth was carried out.

'Don't tell my father that I was here with you.'

Now the lord in green comes out and goes into the stable.

'I know you, young miller! My daughter has been with you.'

'I have not seen your daughter. I know naught! Naught do I know about your daughters!'

The lord went away.

Presently the lord appears again, and he calls: 'I have trees that I want you to fell before midday.'

Now the two go outside so that he may point out the trees, and great trees they were.

'There they are, young miller, dost see them?'

'Yes,' said he. He pulls off his coat. He fells three trees. But there were more standing.

'If I were at home I would die there: but as things are, it is here I must die.' He sat down and began to weep.

The young lady came to him with his dinner. 'Get up' says she, 'and have your dinner.' He ate; he made an end of eating. He stood up and saw the trees were all felled.

'My father will ask you whether I was with you. But you must say "No".' The lady went away.

Now the old lord comes out. 'Yes, young miller! I know that one of my daughters has been with you.'

'Do not lie! I know naught about your daughters – none of them!' The two come back to the castle.

'I want a barn built up yonder,' said the lord – the Green Man of No Man's Land. And the young fellow has to build this barn, and he has to take one feather from every bird to make the thatch. He built the place but the thatch was lacking. He caught one little red bird; he took a single feather from it, and let the little red bird go. He looked at the place. He sat down and knew not what to do. And there he was sitting when the young lady came with his tea.

'Get up and have your tea.' He got up to eat it. He finished. 'The task is done,' she said. Sure enough! The barn was a lovely sight with that feather roof on it – one feather from every bird; all colours! 'Tell my father that you care naught for him or his daughters.'

The lady spoke again: 'There is a mountain in the lake, about a mile out, and a bird will come there and will lay one egg. Tomorrow my father will tell you about it. And you must yourself offer to go and get it. Go to the lake and I will be there.'

The morrow came. The old gentleman told him what he had to do.

'Pooh!' said the young miller, 'that is naught.'

And now here he is by the lake. He sits down. Presently the lady came with his food.

'Pull off one shoe,' says she when he'd done eating. 'Wish that your shoe be turned into a boat.' So it was. Lo! the two get into the boat. And they come to the mountain. He could not climb it.

'Wish my fingers to be turned into a ladder for you to climb up by.' As soon as he said the word, there was the ladder. And the lady said to him:

'When you go up the ladder, pick up each rung one after the other. Do not forget a single one.' He missed one and thus broke one of the lady's fingers. They got the egg. Now the pair are going back.

'Say to my father, when you go back to the castle, and when my father asks whether I have been with you, "No, I know naught about you nor about your daughters".'

The old lord said: 'One of my daughters has been with thee.'

'No,' said the young fellow, 'I have not seen them.'

'I have a little job for you in the morning.'

The young fellow was out betimes and the young lady found him and had a talk with him.

'I have two sisters, and tomorrow my father will once more turn us into three swans. We three sisters will fly over the house three times. And my father will tell you to choose the same one three times. When we fly over the house, you must choose the first one, and when we come back choose the middlemost, and when we come back again choose the last one.'

Morning came. The old lord – the Green Man of No Man's Land – and the young miller were out together in front of the door. Lo! the three big white birds fly over the house.

'I will have the first one.'

Lo! They are returning.

'I will have the middlemost.'

Lo! they are flying back again.

'Which is it now?'

'I will have the last one.' said the young miller to the old lord.

'Yes, thou hast won her: she shall be thy wife.'

Now they are married.

The old lord died; and now the young miller is in the castle.

12

Down Underground

This is a tale that Lander Smith used to tell about himself, an' for foolishness and lies I don't think even Appy Boswell could beat it. He'd get talking about the old lead mining shafts there are in parts o' Derbyshire; sensible talk it would be mind you, to begin with. But after when he'd been talking a bit, he'd start up all of a sudden something like this:

'Once when I was in those parts,' he'd say, 'I was taking a walk over the hills when the dog put up a hare, and with me watching it, an' not looking where I was goin', I tumbled down one of these blessed lead-mine shafts.

'It was only but a very narrow one, just big enough for a man to get down; an' all the while I was fallin' I kept hittin' first agen the one side and then agen the other till I was knocked proper senseless. But at last I come to the bottom, an' right glad I was an' all, you may bet. Every bone in my body felt as if it was broke, but being as I was down underground I think of myself that I might as well see what manner of place it was I'd got to, so I picks myself up and starts out on my travels.

'Everything was different to what it is here. Before long I come to a nice little lake of water, an' there was man with a team of horses ploughing it so that he could plant it with corn. Then I came to a gentleman's park, an' be hanged if there wasn't a ship sailing on the grass and pastures of it.

'And after that I got into a proper main road, and first I met with a donkey riding on a man's back. It was beating him something awful, so I told it if it didn't stop I'd knock its head off; and it *did* stop, leastways as long as I was watching it. Then I lighted on a poor old roadman; he was sitting breaking stones with a feather. And after when I'd left him, I come to a small little house, and there I seen a woman fetching water into a sieve. I was getting a bit hungry by then, so I asked her if she could give me a bite to eat. She said she'd plenty of black puddings if those would do; I said that they'd do fine. So she took me into the garden, an' showed me a tree where there was a wonderful fine crop of these black puddings and she said I could help myself to as many as I pleased.'

I don't know what else he didn't say – Lander, I mean – but the end of it was that there, down underground, he met with some gypsies and came back again with them.

'We had to go over the sea,' he said, 'the way that they took, but come midday, we found a nice place to light a bit of fire and have some vittles. It was pretty near dark when we landed up on this other side and I wondered wherever we'd got to.

'Then I saw some old pot banks and pottery kilns and I says to myself this must be Stoke! An' so it was, right enough. An' there was my old woman waiting for me, and right glad she was to see me when I'd been away for so long.'

13

The King of the Herrings

Somewhere very far away lived a quarryman. He was old and his wife had never borne him any children. At last a son was born to them, and all the neighbours were amazed – the man and woman were so old to have a child!

The father died and the son took his place. And lo! an old man passes by and the youth looks long at him. Now the old man says:

'Will you come with me to find a living for the two of us?'

'Yes,' says Jack.

'Then say that you wish me turned into an old horse.'

'Done!' says the young fellow. No sooner had he said that than an old horse stood before him with his head hanging down.

'Get on my back; let us be off,' said the horse.

So off they set, the old horse – the nag – and Jack, along the road. Said the old nag to the lad:

'If you should chance to see or hear anyone in

trouble on the way, go and find out what is the matter, and if you can do anything, then do it.'

Lo and behold! Here we are upon the road. And here we are taking the hill! And now the pair are well on their way, not far from the sea.

Said Jack to the nag, 'I hear something.'

'Go and see what it is.'

He got down from the horse's back to see what was there. He saw a little herring that the tide had left stranded. He picked it up and put it in the water. And lo! the fish swam right up to him.

Said the fish to Jack: 'Whatever I can do for you, call upon "The King of the Herrings" – and I will do it.'

Jack says goodbye and walks back to his horse and away they go over the hill.

'Jack, touch nothing that you see, even though it is the finest thing you have ever seen,' said the old horse.

And lo! The wind blew a feather – a quill – into Jack's mouth.

Twice or thrice he spat it out. Back came the quill-feather again. He thought it was pretty and so he put it in his pocket.

And now they come to an old castle. And they hear a great roaring and shouting inside this castle.

'Go and see what is the matter,' said the old nag.

Jack went up to the castle and knocked at the gate. No one came out to him. He opened the gate and went in to see what was happening. He found the uproar was from a giant lying on a bed – helpless. That giant could do nothing for himself: he was ill. There was no maid-servant to give him food.

'What ails you, friend?'

'I have no serving wench in this place. Go, bring me food and a tankard of ale from below.'

The giant ate and drank his fill and told Jack to call on him if ever he could do anything for him. Off goes the lad on his old horse again. Now the pair are going downhill.

Said the old nag, 'What did you see when we were on the mountain?'

'I saw nothing but a little feather which the wind blew into my mouth.'

'Did you take the feather?'

'Yes, I have it in my pocket.'

'This feather will bring us misfortune, but, now you've got it, keep it; do not let it go.'

And now the young man goes to a grand mansion to look for work. The master of the house came outside to see if he could write. Jack's writing was excellent. You could not beat it.

Then the lad thought he had better go in search of somewhere to sleep. The master invited him to sleep in the house.

'Nay,' said Jack, 'I will go out to my old nag in the stable.'

Everyone marvelled at his feats with this feather that had blown into his mouth.

One day the manservant said to his master. 'Call the young fellow hither, master, so that while he is with you I may get hold of his feather – his quill.'

The master called Jack. He came. The servant took away his quill feather and put another on his writing table.

'Master, I have it,' says the servant, and went on: 'The man who brought the feather can bring the bird too.'

Said Jack to the old nag: 'The master wants the bird.'

'Go and ask him to give you three days and three purses of gold.'

They went off in search of the bird.

'Jack, go up to that castle yonder and walk in. You will see a company feasting at table. Touch nothing. In a corner you will see a draggle-tailed bird in a cage. Go and take it, but don't linger.'

Out comes Jack to the old nag carrying the bird.

The pair are back, bringing the bird with them. Soon the master and his servant talked all this over as they looked at the bird.

The servant said to the master:

'The bird is pretty; the lady is prettier still; And the man who brought the bird here can bring the lady too.'

Jack went out to the old nag and told him that now the master wanted the lady.

'I warned you about the feather, Jack. Go and ask him for three days and three purses of gold.'

Jack went back to ask. He got the money and the three days. Away they go!

They talk together on the road. Down by the sea the road went. Says the old nag to Jack, 'Jack, wish me turned into a ship of the sea.'

As soon as the word was spoken there was the ship on the sea. And here he is going aboard. That ship was laden with silk. Now they are sailing under cliffs on which a castle stands.

'Jack! Go up to the castle and ask to see the lady. She whom you will see coming out to you is not the lady; ask to see the lady herself.'

Jack went to the castle. He knocked at the gate, and lo! a lady appears. She was not the mistress, she was the housekeeper.

Said Jack to her, 'I want to see the lady herself.'

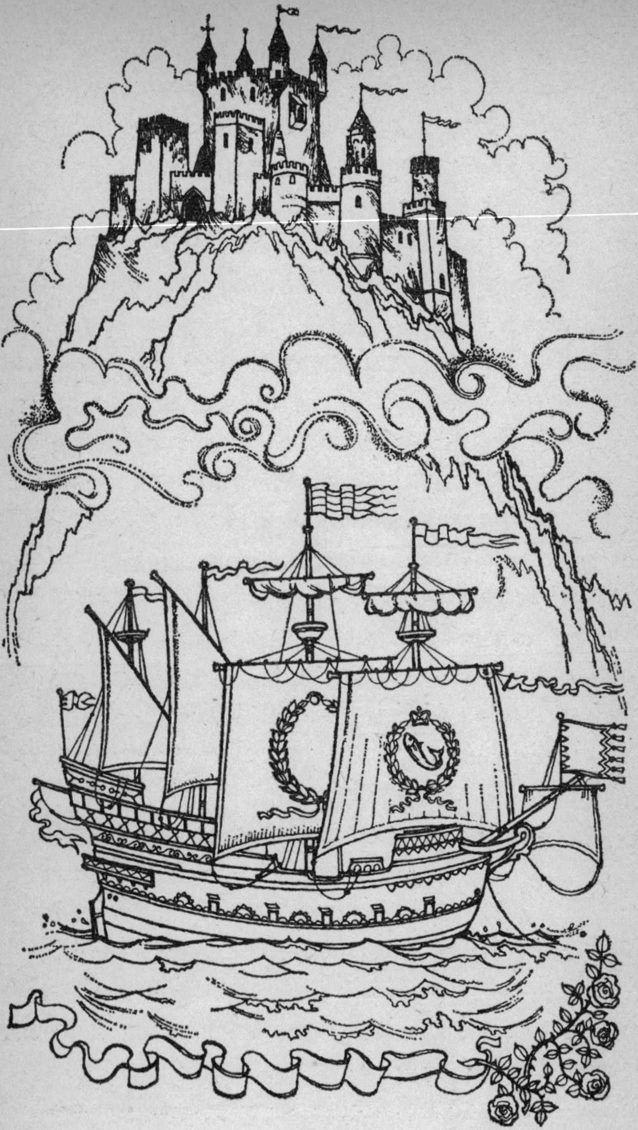

The housekeeper went in to tell her mistress. Soon the lady came out. Jack told her there was a ship laden with silk at anchor below the castle; she stepped down to look, and saw the ship. The lady came aboard and one of the crew led her to where the silk was stored. Jack stayed on deck. He weighed anchor and the ship sailed away.

And now they are far out at sea. By this time the lady had finished her business and came out on deck. When she saw that she had been trapped, she felt in her pocket, pulled out her keys and flung them into the sea. The sea turned red as blood and was troubled by a mighty storm; but in spite of that they sailed on . . .

Here they are back at the mansion! And Jack leads the lady inside. Soon the master and servant speak a few words together. Says the servant to his master: 'The man who brought the lady here can bring the castle too.'

Jack went out to the old nag and told him.

'Well, Jack, I warned you about the feather – that it would bring us misfortune. Go back and ask him for three days and three sacks of gold.'

Jack went back and got them. When they were both well on their way, the old nag asked Jack, 'What did the giant say to you?'

'He promised he would do anything for me.'

They sailed under a cliff on which a castle stood

'Go to him and tell him what you want.'

So up Jack goes to the giant's castle. He told the giant what he wanted, and the giant fell a-laughing at him. He sent him out to fetch his chain, but Jack could not lift a single link. Again the giant burst out laughing, and straightway strode out, picked up the chain, and slung it over his shoulder. Now they both go down to the lady's castle. The giant fastened the chain to the castle, put it on his back and carried it down to the lady's biding place. There was a high wall round the lady's home and the gate was locked.

Said the lady to Jack, 'I want my keys: I cannot open the gate.'

Again Jack went out to consult the old nag. 'Jack, I warned you about that feather!'

So here they are again journeying along the road.

'Jack, what did that little herring say to you?'

'Whatever I can do for you, I will do: should you have need of me, you must call upon "The King of the Herrings".'

Jack and the old nag made for the spot where the road led down by the sea, where he had found the fish, and now he hailed him. Lo! the fish swam up to him. Jack told him about the lady's keys.

'I will go in search of them, Jack.' The little

herring disappeared and was gone a great while. He came back but he hadn't found the keys.

'I have not found them, Jack, but I will try again.'

And again he was gone a great while. At last he reappeared and he had found the keys and he gave them to Jack. The herring swam away and the old nag and Jack went home. Jack handed the keys to the lady.

The lady asked Jack, 'Which would you rather, Jack, that your head or that your master's head be cut off?'

Jack stopped to think what answer he should make. Then he said to the lady, 'Do not slay him, slay me.'

Said the lady: 'You have spoken well, Jack; you have answered well. If you had not spoken thus you would have been killed. Now it is your master who will be killed.'

Jack and the lady were married and the master was slain. And the lady and Jack still live in the castle.

14

The Red King and the Witch

It was the Red King, and he went to the market, bought enough food for two weeks, cooked it, and put it in a cupboard. Then he locked the cupboard and posted people to guard it.

In the morning, when he looked, he found the platters bare; he did not find anything on them. Then the King said:

'I will give half my kingdom to whoever can be found to guard the cupboard, that the victuals may not go a-missing from it.'

The King had three sons. The eldest thought within himself: 'What? Give half the kingdom to a stranger? It would be better for me to watch.'

He went to his father: 'Father, all hail. What? Give half the kingdom to a stranger? It would be better for me to watch.'

And his father said to him: 'Very well, only don't be frightened by what you see.'

So the young man went and lay down in the

room in the palace where the cupboard was. And he put his head on the pillow and there he lay until towards dawn. And a warm, sleepy breeze came and lulled him to sleep. His little sister lay in her cradle in the same room. She got up and she turned a somersault and her nails became like an axe and her teeth like a shovel. She opened the cupboard and ate up everything. Then she became a little child again and returned to her place in the cradle.

The lad arose and told his father that he had seen nothing. His father looked in the cupboard, found the platters bare – no victuals! No anything!

His father said, 'It would take a better man than you, and even he might do nothing.' Once more the King put food on the platters.

So now his middle son said, 'Father, all hail! I am going to watch tonight.'

'Go dear, play the man.'

And he went into the palace and put his head on a pillow. There came a warm breeze and sleep seized him. Up rose his little sister, and unwound herself from her swaddling bands, and turned a somersault, and her teeth became like a shovel and her nails like an axe. And she went to the cupboard and opened it, and ate off the platters all that she found. She ate it all, and turned a somersault and went back to her place in the cradle. Day broke and the lad arose, but the King saw that the food had gone.

So the youngest son, Peterkin, said, 'Father, all hail. Give me also leave to watch the cupboard by night.'

'Go, dear, only don't be frightened with what you see.'

And the lad went and took four needles with him and lay down with his head on the pillow; and he stuck the four needles into the pillow in four places. When sleep seized him he knocked his head against a needle, so he stayed awake.

And his little sister arose from her cradle, and he saw. And she turned a somersault, and he was watching her. And her teeth became like a shovel and her nails like an axe, and he saw that too. And she went to the cupboard and ate up everything. She left the platters bare. And she turned a somersault, and became a child again as she was, and went to her cradle. The lad, when he saw that, trembled with fear; it seemed to him ten years till daybreak. And he arose and went to his father.

'Father, all hail.'

Then his father asked him, 'Did you see anything, Peterkin?'

'What did I see? What did I not see?' said

Peterkin. 'Here I will not stay, give me money and a horse.'

His father gave him a couple of sacks of silver money, and he put them on his horse and led the horse outside the city. The lad made a chest of stone, and put all the money there, and buried it there – outside the city. He put up a stone cross above, and off he rode. And he journeyed and at last he came to the Queen of all the birds that fly.

And the Queen of the Birds asked him, 'Whither away, Peterkin?'

'I'm going to where there is neither death nor old age, and there I shall find a wife.'

'Here is neither death nor old age,' said the Queen.

'How comes it that here is neither death nor old age?' Peterkin said to her.

'Not till I whittle away the wood of all this forest,' said she, 'will death come and old age overtake me.'

'One day and one morning death will come and old age, and take me,' Peterkin said.

So he would not stay with the Queen of the Birds, but went further, and journeyed on. He arrived at a palace made of copper that stood among many mountains. And a maiden came forth from the palace and took him by the hand

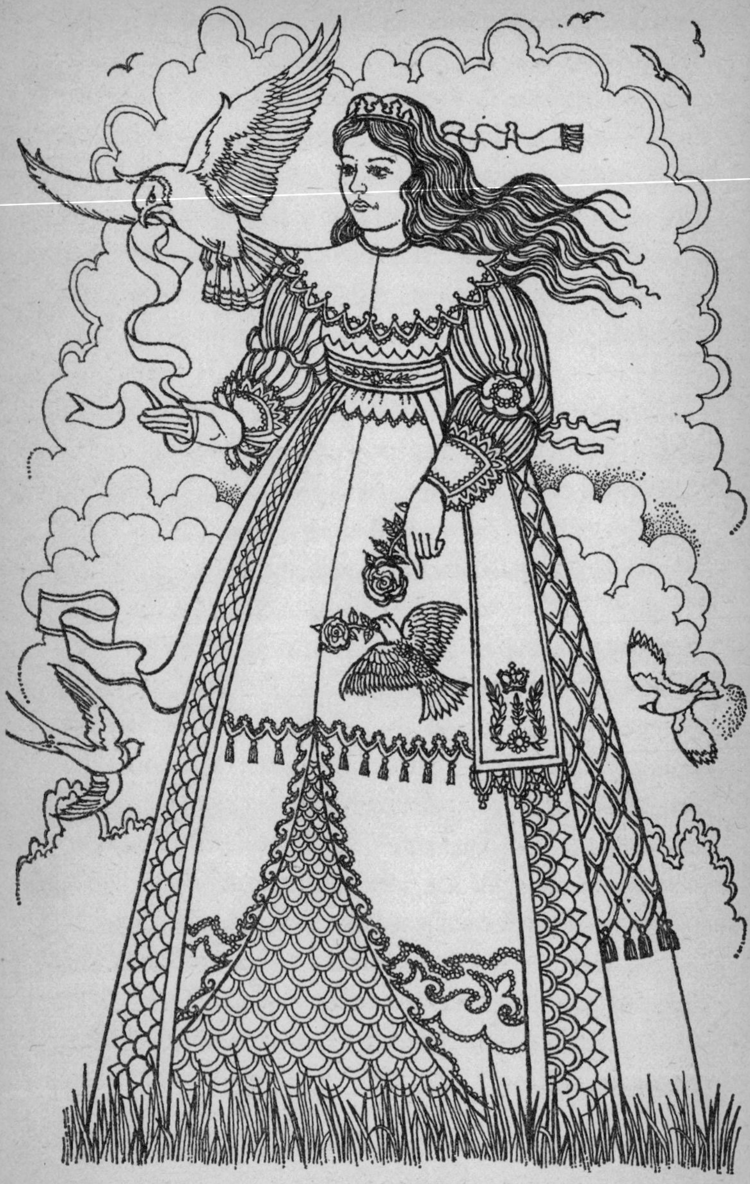

and kissed him. She said, 'I have waited long for you.'

She took the horse and put him in the stable, and the lad spent the night there. He arose in the morning and put his saddle on the horse. Then the maiden began to cry, and asked him, 'Why are you going away, Peterkin?'

'I am going to where there is neither death nor old age.'

'Here is neither death nor old age,' the maiden said to him.

'How comes it that here there is neither death nor old age?'

'Not till all these mountains are levelled will death come,' said she.

'This is no place for me,' said Peterkin, and he departed further.

Then what did his horse say to him? 'Master, whip me four times, and twice yourself, for we have come to the Plain of Regret. Ride quickly, for if you linger Regret will seize you and cast you down, horse and all. So escape and tarry not.'

Peterkin did as the horse said. He rode over the plain without looking to right or left.

He came to a hut. In that hut he sees a young boy, as it were, ten years old.

'Why have you come here, Peterkin, and what are you looking for?' asked the boy.

He came at last to the Queen of all the birds

'I am looking for the place where there is neither death nor old age.'

'Here is neither death nor old age. I am The Wind!' answered the boy.

Then Peterkin said, 'Never, never will I go away from this place.'

And he lived there a million years and grew no older.

Sometimes he went into the Mountains of Gold and Silver to hunt, and found so much game there that he could scarcely carry it all back.

Then what said The Wind to him?

'Peterkin, go as much as you like to the Mountains of Gold and Silver, but never go to the Plain of Regret or to the Mountain of Grief.'

But Peterkin did not heed what The Wind told him, and one day he went far. He went beyond the Mountain of Gold and Silver to the Mountain of Grief and to the Plain of Regret. And Regret and Grief cast him down; he wept till his eyes were full.

When he got back he went to The Wind.

'I am going home to my father; I will stay no longer.'

'Do not go, for your father is dead,' said the boy – The Wind, 'and so are your brothers. A million years have come and gone since you rode away. The spot is not known,' said The Wind, 'where your father's palace stood. They have planted melons on it; I know this because it is only an hour since I passed that way.'

But Peterkin would not heed. He departed, and arrived and saw the maiden to whom the Palace of Copper belonged. Only one small mound was left of all those mountains, and she dug away one more spadeful, and grew old. As he knocked at the door, she died. He buried her and departed thence.

And he came to the Queen of the Birds in the place of the great forest. Only one tree remained of all that forest – a tree with only one branch on it, and that was all but cut through.

When she saw him, the Queen said, 'Peterkin, you are still quite young!'

'Do you remember telling me to tarry here?' Peterkin said to her.

She pressed and whittled and she broke through the branch, and then she too fell and died.

He journeyed on and at last he came to where his father's palace had stood, and there he looked about him. There was no palace, no anything. And he fell to marvelling. He thought he recognized his father's well, and went to it. His sister, the witch, was still there, and when she saw him she said to him, 'I have waited long for you, dog!' and with that, she rushed at him, meaning to eat him, but he made the sign of the cross and she perished.

Peterkin saw that standing near was an old man with his beard down to his belt.

'Father,' said Peterkin, 'where is the palace of the Red King? I am his son.'

'What is this?' said the old man, 'you tell me that you, who are still a youth, are the son of the Red King? My father's father told me of the Red King. His very city is no more. And you tell me that you are his son!'

'It is not twenty years, old man,' said Peterkin, 'since I left home, and you tell me that you don't know my father?'

(It was a million years since he had left home.)

'Follow me, if you don't believe me,' Peterkin went on.

So they went out to the cross of stone; only a palm's breadth was out of the ground. And it took Peterkin two days' digging to get at the chest of money. When he had lifted the chest out, he opened it.

Death sat in one corner groaning, and Old Age sat groaning in another corner.

Then what said Old Age?

'Lay hold of him, Death.'

'Lay hold of him yourself.'

Old Age laid hold of him in front, and Death laid hold of him behind.

When it was all over with Peterkin, the old man buried him decently, planted the stone cross near him, and took the money and also the horse.

Afterword

As you read these stories you may have noticed that they seemed like stories being told out loud and not at all like 'written' stories. This is because the tales in the book are set out just as they were told by very old Gypsies, who often didn't know how to read or write. For generations these stories were handed down from mouth-to-mouth until people grew interested in such old tales and took them down more or less word for word. Most of these were written down either by Professor Sampson or Miss Dora Yates about fifty years ago, and nearly all these particular stories were collected in Wales.

George Borrow, about 100 years ago, wrote: 'A very remarkable set of people are the Gypsies . . . and they speak a language of their own.' Borrow was a learned man, who could speak six or seven languages, including the Gypsy's Romany. He travelled about Britain and Spain on foot for years, often with the Gypsies. Here is what he says about where Gypsies come from:

'Gypsies sometimes said that they came from Lower Egypt and were doing penance by a seven years wandering for the sins of their forefathers, who of old had refused hospitality to the Virgin Mary. But they were not really from Egypt, but from a much more distant land – India. They came to Britain, Spain and Russia with their horses, donkeys and tilted carts. The "Romany Chals" (the name in which British Gypsies delight) means "Lads of Rama" (an Indian God), or else "Lads of Rome" (the city).'

In England you often find that a copse or a lane is mysteriously called 'Engine Copse' or 'Engine Lane'. 'Engine' here does not mean 'Traction Engine', or indeed anything in that line. It means 'Egyptian' or 'Indian' – that is, a place where Gypsies often camped.

Borrow also quotes a saying which became famous as a description of what Gypsies think. It was said, so he tells us, by an old Gypsy man.

'There's Day and Night, Brother, both sweet things;
Sun, Moon and Stars, Brother, all sweet things.
There's likewise the wind on the heath.
Life is very sweet, Brother; who would wish to die?'

There was only one Gypsy that I myself knew at all well. He was called Uriah Lovell, a most courtly and accomplished old man. He made his living by weaving baskets and the like and would talk as he worked in a sweet, low voice. He lived in a little plaited wigwam and kept his camp scrupulously clean and neat. He was very handsome with short, curly grey hair and gold earrings, and he often wore a brilliant yellow silk scarf. He kept himself to himself and yet was always friendly, and he would sometimes say in his reflective way that he was probably as happy as a man could possibly be.

There is something fascinating about Gypsy names. I knew of one half Gypsy whose name was Noah. Trafalgar is another Gypsy (boy's) name. Cinderella is a girl's name, and there was once a Gypsy called 'Noname'. His mother had wanted to have him named Jehovah, and when the clergyman refused, he was Christened 'Noname' instead.

There's a book about Gypsies that I read recently, *The Book of Boswell: The Autobiography of a Gypsy*, by Silvester Gordon Boswell (Gollancz 1970). Ask for it at your library. It was dictated to a writer called John Seymour.

Mr Boswell is a modern Gypsy, and is in a big way of business as a scrap merchant, owning big cranes and lorries worth a couple of thousand pounds each. He has a large family, and his wife is called Athaliah. He said of one of his sons – Lewis:

'Lewis is the typical Gypsy-man. More of a Gypsy-man than anyone left in the family, and I think he intends to lead the Gypsy life as much as he can and as much as he *dare*. Although that's difficult at times, even for him. He loves his stick fire, he loves his green grass, exactly like me, he will never settle. I don't think so! I can't see him settling – he's not that type; he doesn't want to and his wife doesn't. So I think that's good.'

I believe we ought to be careful how we try to make Gypsies settled and tidy – we ought to prevent their being pushed off the roads and driven away from their camping places.

AMABEL WILLIAMS-ELLIS

Notes

The Leaves that Hung but Never Grew (page 7)
What are these mysterious leaves? These stories may well be Medieval and certainly came from a time when

most Gypsies could neither read nor write. I suspect that the leaves 'never grew' because they weren't tree leaves.

In late Medieval times when printing was first invented, paper makers and printers hung their 'leaves' up to dry. Printed words were (and still are) often thought by people who couldn't read to be magical. So could these have been printed paper 'leaves'? Perhaps pages from a legal document that the nobleman wanted so that his daughter could inherit his property? Or perhaps they might have been pages from a book of magic?

I don't know really – this is just an idea of mine.

AMABEL WILLIAMS-ELLIS

The Red King and the Witch (page 114)

This Rumanian Gypsy story seems to me to be like Albrecht Dürer's 'Knight' or the *csardas* of some great Gypsy maestro. There are several non-Gypsy stories that offer striking analogies, so that it would not be difficult to patch together a story that would almost exactly parallel this Gypsy one. 'Rip Van Winkle' is only one of many tales or ballads from many countries whose main theme is the same – that of the relativity of Time. But to the present writer this Gypsy tale seems to be one of the best of an impressive lot.

FRANCIS HINDES-GROOME